STUDENT UNIT

NEW EDITION

AQA A2 Law Unit 3

Criminal Law (Offences Against the Person) and Contract Law

Peter Darwent and Ian Yule

Philip Allan, an imprint of Hodder Education, an Hachette UK company, Market Place, Deddington, Oxfordshire OX15 0SE

Orders
Bookpoint Ltd, 130 Milton Park, Abingdon, Oxfordshire OX14 4SB
tel: 01235 827827
fax: 01235 400401
e-mail: education@bookpoint.co.uk
Lines are open 9.00 a.m.–5.00 p.m., Monday to Saturday, with a 24-hour message answering service. You can also order through the Philip Allan website: www.philipallan.co.uk

© Peter Darwent and Ian Yule 2013

ISBN 978-1-4441-7373-4

First printed 2013
Impression number 5 4 3 2 1
Year 2016 2015 2014 2013

Cover photo: blas/Fotolia

AQA examination questions are reproduced by permission of the Assessment and Qualifications Alliance

Typeset by Integra Software Services Pvt. Ltd., Pondicherry, India

Printed in Dubai

Hachette UK's policy is to use papers that are natural, renewable and recyclable products and made from wood grown in sustainable forests. The logging and manufacturing processes are expected to conform to the environmental regulations of the country of origin.

P2171

Contents

Content Guidance

Section A: Criminal law (offences against the person)

Section B: Contract law

Questions and Answers

Section A

Section B

Getting the most from this book

Examiner tips
Advice from the examiner on key points in the text to help you learn and recall unit content, avoid pitfalls, and polish your exam technique in order to boost your grade.

Knowledge check
Rapid-fire questions throughout the Content Guidance section to check your understanding.

Knowledge check answers
1 Turn to the back of the book for the Knowledge check answers.

Summaries
● Each core topic is rounded off by a bullet-list summary for quick-check reference of what you need to know.

Questions & Answers

Exam-style questions

Examiner comments on the questions
Tips on what you need to do to gain full marks, indicated by the icon **e**.

Sample student answers
Practise the questions, then look at the student answers that follow each set of questions.

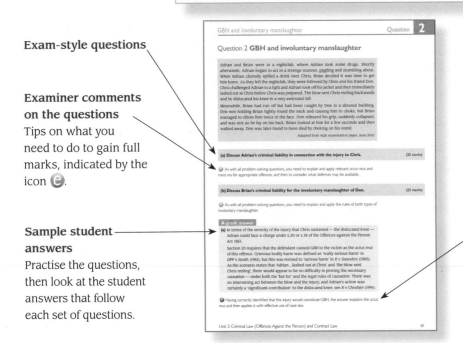

Examiner commentary on sample student answers
Find out how many marks each answer would be awarded in the exam and then read the examiner comments (preceded by the icon **e**) following each student answer.

About this book

The AQA specification for the A2 Law examinations is divided into two units. This guide covers Unit 3. Section A is Criminal Law (Offences against the Person) and Section B is Contract Law. For each section, the examination offers two three-part questions, and from these you select just one question to answer. The first two parts of each question are based on a scenario, and deal with substantive law issues; the third part is evaluative, and you are required to analyse aspects of either criminal law or contract law to consider potential criticisms, and possibly to suggest how the law could be reformed.

For the substantive law part of the module, it is vital to use case law effectively, and in the Questions and Answers section of this guide, you will be shown how best to employ case and statutory references.

This guide is divided into two sections: Content Guidance and Questions and Answers. The Content Guidance section sets out the specification content for this unit, breaking it down into manageable areas for study and learning. It also contains references to case law to enable a fuller understanding of each topic. This section is not intended to be a comprehensive and detailed set of notes for this unit. You will need to supplement this material with further reading from textbooks and case studies.

The Questions and Answers section encourages you to test yourself. If you practise answering the sample questions and then assess your responses against the examiner's comments, you will learn how to use your knowledge and understanding more effectively to obtain high exam marks.

The key to doing well in the criminal law part of this unit lies in acquiring the ability to identify the appropriate offences and defences, and then defining the *actus reus* and *mens rea* of these, plus the defence requirements, and finally using relevant cases. For contract law, you need to be able to identify relevant issues on offer, acceptance, breach and remedies. To demonstrate a sound understanding of potential content, you need to practise answering past examination questions.

It is particularly important that you are able to apply legal rules to the specific scenario-based questions. This has been identified as a key examination weakness in successive examiner's reports.

Content Guidance

Section A: Criminal law (offences against the person)

Summary of non-fatal offences

These should be thoroughly revised from Unit 2. Pay particular attention to the examiner tips.

One of the two questions in each scenario will always involve non-fatal offences. Often the scenarios are complex and may require discussion of two or more offences as well as a possible defence.

Assault

Examiner tip
Ensure that you can explain *and* apply the *actus reus* and *mens rea* rules.

The *actus reus* is any act which makes the victim fear the immediate infliction of unlawful force. In *Smith* v *Woking Police* (1983) it was looking at a woman in her night clothes through a window. In *Lamb* there was no assault because the victim did not fear the immediate infliction of force. Words alone could be enough and even a silent phone call (*Ireland*, 1997). In *Constanza* (1997) letters sent by a stalker were interpreted as clear threats and there was 'fear of violence at some time not excluding the immediate future'. Words can also annul assault (*Tuberville* v *Savage*, 1669).

The *mens rea* is intention to create fear or subjective recklessness (*Cunningham*, 1957) — you know there is an unjustified risk that fear will be created.

Battery

The *actus reus* is the application of unlawful force. There is no need to prove harm or pain. A mere touch can be sufficient, such as tickling or kissing. Any unlawful physical contact is technically battery. In *Collins* v *Willcocks* (1984) it was held that 'any touching of another person, however slight, may amount to a battery' but it is now accepted that the contact must be hostile — *Wilson* v *Pringle* (1986). Scratches and minor bruising are likely to be treated as battery, although there is no need for injury to be proved.

It can be indirect — in *DPP* v *K* it was battery when acid was put in a hot air hand drier and injured someone. In *Haystead* (2000) it was battery on a baby when a man punched a woman, causing her to drop the baby.

The *mens rea* is intention or *Cunningham* (subjective) recklessness as to whether unlawful force will be applied — *Venna* (1976).

ABH s.47 Offences Against the Person Act 1861

This is defined in the Act as 'any assault occasioning actual bodily harm'. The *actus reus* is either assault or battery plus actual bodily harm. In *Miller* (1954) ABH includes 'any hurt or injury calculated to interfere with health or comfort', but it has to be more than 'transient or trifling'. Harm is not limited to injury to the skin, flesh and bones. In *Smith* v *DPP* it was held that cutting off a girl's ponytail amounted to ABH.

It can include psychiatric injury, but in *Chan Fook* (1994) it was said that psychiatric injury 'does not include mere emotions such as fear or distress or panic'. There must be 'some identifiable clinical condition'.

Only the *mens rea* for assault or battery is needed. For example, in *Roberts* (1971) a man gave a girl a lift in his car and made sexual advances, touching her clothes. She feared rape and jumped from the moving car and was injured. He argued that he saw no risk of injury, but the court said that it was sufficient that he had the *mens rea* for battery. Another example is *Savage* (1992).

Wounding and GBH s.20

This is defined as 'unlawfully and maliciously wounding or inflicting any grievous bodily harm upon any other person either with or without a weapon'.

The *actus reus* is either inflicting GBH or wounding. GBH means serious harm (*Saunders*, 1985). Wounding means breaking the skin, not internal bleeding as in *C (a minor)* v *Eisenhower* (1984). Technically, some of the things charged as ABH or indeed any injury that breaks the skin could amount to wounding and be charged under s.20. It can include psychiatric injury as long as it is 'serious' (*Ireland* and *Burstow*, 1997). Inflict does not require direct contact (confirmed in *Burstow*) and therefore means the same as cause in s.18.

The *mens rea* is intention or *Cunningham* recklessness as to whether *some* harm is caused. In *Mowatt* (1968) it was confirmed that the defendant merely has to foresee some physical harm, albeit of a minor character.

Wounding and GBH s.18

The *actus reus* of this offence is identical to that of s.20 — wounding or causing GBH. The difference between the two offences is entirely in the *mens rea*.

The *mens rea* of s.18 is either intention to cause GBH or intention to resist arrest. Intention can be direct or oblique, which is where you claim to have some other purpose, but the jury are satisfied that you knew serious injury was virtually certain (*Nedrick/Woollin*).

Fatal offences against the person

Murder

Murder is the most serious crime against the person, and the offender, if convicted, will receive a mandatory life sentence. Murder is defined as 'unlawful killing with

Examiner tip

In problem-solving questions, ensure that you are able to identify the correct level of offence to 'match' the seriousness of the injury. A common problem is to select s.47 ABH even when a serious injury or a wound has occurred which should be s.20 (or even s.18). In such cases, the mark scheme sets a limit of 'max. clear'.

Examiner tip

In questions involving GBH and/or wounding, unless a weapon has been used, discuss s.20 first and decide whether the *actus reus* and *mens rea* have been met. If time permits, give some consideration to the possibility of a s.18 offence.

malice aforethought'. The *actus reus* is unlawful killing and the *mens rea* — malice aforethought — is more clearly defined as intention to kill or commit grievous bodily harm (GBH).

Actus reus

The *actus reus* often requires the examination of various rules of causation, in order to establish whether the defendant caused or brought about the death of the victim, hence the need to revise this topic thoroughly from Unit 2.

Mens rea

The *mens rea* for murder is malice aforethought, meaning intention to kill or commit GBH. The meaning of intention is found not in any statute but in judicial decisions. It is clear that a person intends a result when it is his or her aim, objective or purpose to bring it about — this is what might be termed 'dictionary intention'. In *R v Mohan* (1976), James LJ stated:

> An 'intention', to my mind, connotes a state of affairs which the party intending...does more than merely contemplate. It connotes a state of affairs which, on the contrary, he decides, so far as in him lies, to bring about, and which, in point of possibility, he has a reasonable prospect of being able to bring about by his own act of volition.

In the case of *R v Hancock and Shankland* (1986), this issue was at the heart of the case. The judges had to decide how the law should deal with a defendant who has created an unlawful result where it is clear that the outcome was probable — even highly probable — and the defendant may well have foreseen this outcome.

The defendants were convicted of murder at their trial, but the Court of Appeal and House of Lords both quashed those convictions and substituted manslaughter convictions, holding that the issue of intention had not been established. Lord Scarman indicated that, in cases like these, juries needed to be told by the judge that 'the greater the probability of a consequence occurring, the more likely it was so foreseen and, if so, the more likely it was intended'. This emphasised that foresight of a degree of probability was only evidence from which intention could be inferred.

In the more recent cases of *R v Nedrick* (1986) and R v *Woollin* (1998), a tighter rule was laid down for such cases of oblique intent. This rule provides that juries may return a verdict of murder only where they find that 'the defendant foresaw death or serious injury as a virtually certain consequence of his or her voluntary actions'. In both these cases, the original murder conviction was substituted on appeal by a manslaughter conviction.

In *R v Woollin* (1998), the defendant initially gave a number of different explanations, but finally admitted that he had 'lost his cool' when his 3-month-old baby son started to choke on his food. He had shaken the baby and then, in a fit of rage or frustration, had thrown him in the direction of his pram, which was standing against the wall about a metre away. He knew that the baby's head had hit something hard but denied intending to throw him against the wall or wanting him to die or suffer serious injury. The trial judge did not direct the jury to deal with the issue of intention on the basis of the *Nedrick* 'foresight of virtually certain consequences' rule and the defendant was convicted of murder. The Court of Appeal, although critical of the trial judge, dismissed the appeal, and certified questions for the House of Lords. The House of Lords quashed the defendant's conviction for murder and substituted a conviction for manslaughter. Lord Steyn, who gave the main speech, held that 'a result foreseen as virtually certain is an intended result'.

In *R v Matthews and Alleyne* (2003), the defendants had robbed a student and then, knowing that he could not swim, they threw him into the Thames where he drowned. It was held, confirming their murder conviction, that the 'virtual certainty' rule was evidential, not substantive, but that in practice there was very little difference between a rule of evidence and a rule of substantive law.

Voluntary manslaughter

Voluntary manslaughter covers the situation where the defendant has committed the *actus reus* of murder (unlawful killing) with the required *mens rea* (specific intention to kill or commit GBH) but there are extenuating circumstances that reduce the defendant's liability. These circumstances operate as partial defences, and are defined as loss of control or diminished responsibility.

The basis of all serious criminal liability — the liability to be prosecuted and, if convicted, to be punished — rests on the principle of fault. In the case of these partial defences, which can only be pleaded to a murder charge, the law recognises that, in some way, the defendant's fault has been reduced and therefore he or she is entitled to receive a lower punishment than life imprisonment.

Diminished responsibility

The new rules on diminished responsibility are contained in the **Coroners and Justice Act 2009** which came into effect in October 2010. These new rules directly substitute the former rules under s.2 of the **Homicide Act 1957**, which therefore remains the authority for this defence.

Under s.52 of the 2009 Act substitute for existing s.2 of the Homicide Act 1957 the requirements for these new rules are that the defendant (D) must have been suffering from an abnormality of mental functioning which:

(a) arose from a recognised medical condition, which
(b) substantially impaired D's ability to do one or more of the things mentioned in subsection (1A), and
(c) provides an explanation for D's acts and omissions in doing or being a party to the killing

Those things are:
(a) to understand the nature of D's conduct
(b) to form a rational judgement
(c) to exercise self-control

The first requirement is that the defendant has to be able to prove — on the balance of probabilities — that he or she was suffering from an abnormality of mental functioning that arose from a recognised medical condition. This is a more stringent test than the previous requirement of 'abnormality of mind', which was heavily criticised as being more of a legal test than a psychiatric test. The new test requires psychiatrists to provide a medical diagnosis in terms of a *recognised* medical condition.

Knowledge check 1

What is the rule for oblique intent from the cases of *Nedrick* and *Woollin*?

Examiner tip

In a murder question, especially if there are no causation issues, you should include an analysis of oblique intent and discuss whether the defendant may be convicted of murder through the use of this rule — 'foresight of death or serious injury as virtually certain'.

Knowledge check 2

Which Act is the authority for diminished responsibility?

Under the former rules which required an abnormality of mind, the Byrne Test was used — juries had to ask whether the defendant's state of mind was so different from the normal person that any reasonable person would term it abnormal. As the new test requires the defendant not only to prove that he or she was suffering from an abnormality of mental functioning arising from a recognised medical condition but also that this substantially impaired the ability to understand the nature of his/her conduct, or to form a rational judgement, or to exercise self-control, it could be argued that the Byrne test is no longer relevant.

It is also clear that the defendant must prove not only that he or she is suffering from an abnormality of mental functioning caused by a recognised medical condition but also that this resulted in a substantial impairment of the ability to do any of the three things in subsection 1A above. This will obviously depend on expert psychiatric testimony. This is a separate test as it would be possible for some psychiatric conditions such as depression not to cause any substantial impairment in these required criteria.

However, it seems clear that there could not be a substantial impairment of mental functioning in one of the specified ways, from a recognised medical condition, without there also being an abnormality of mental functioning.

The new rules — dependent on there being a recognised medical condition — will clearly include untreatable personality disorders which formerly were difficult to include in the 'abnormality of mind' definition as these are contained in the WHO classification of psychiatric conditions.

On the issue of what constitutes 'substantial' impairment, in the absence of any new case authorities on this specific point, it could be argued that the decision in *R* v *Lloyd* (1967) will continue in force that 'the impairment need not be total but it must be more than trivial or minimal'.

Effect of intoxication on diminished responsibility

Where intoxication has produced an abnormality of mental functioning, for example the brain has been damaged because the defendant is an alcoholic, then this element of diminished responsibility could be established. However, for alcohol simply to have had a transitory effect on the mind would not be enough to trigger this defence. In the leading case of *R* v *Tandy* (1989), the Court of Appeal held that for alcohol to produce an abnormality of mind:

> ...the alcoholism had to have reached such a level that the defendant's brain was damaged so that there was gross impairment of his judgement and emotional responses or the craving for drink had to be such as to render the defendant's use of drink involuntary because he was no longer able to resist the impulse to drink.

It is, however, quite possible that the argument made by the then Lord Justice (now Lord Chief Justice) Judge in *R* v *Wood* (2008) that 'as a matter of practical reality the bar the defendant is required to surmount before diminished responsibility can be established in the context of chronic addiction to alcohol may have been set too high' will be dealt with under these new rules as it will be easier for expert psychiatric witnesses to identify whether or not the defendant's alcohol addiction or dependency arose from a 'recognised medical condition'.

Knowledge check 3

List the three requirements for diminished responsibility.

Examiner tip

In any question where the defendant's mental condition could give rise to this defence, the issue of 'substantial impairment' will require explanation and *some attempt* at application.

Knowledge check 4

What was the effect of the decision in *R* v *Tandy*?

The decision in *R v Dietschmann* (2003) seems certain to be unaffected by the new rules in the 2009 Act. In this case, the defendant had killed his victim while intoxicated but also suffering from an abnormality of mind. It was held that, where a defendant was suffering from an abnormality of mind and had also consumed alcohol (and where, as in that case, there was no evidence capable of establishing alcohol dependence syndrome as an abnormality of mind), if he or she satisfies the jury that, ignoring the alcohol consumed and the effect upon him or her, his or her abnormality of mental functioning substantially impaired his or her ability to understand the nature of his or her conduct or to form a rational judgement or to exercise self-control, the jury will find the defendant not guilty of murder but guilty instead of voluntary manslaughter by reason of diminished responsibility.

In conclusion, it appears that under the new rules on diminished responsibility, you will be able in a problem-solving question to explain each of these rules — (1) abnormality of mental functioning which (2) arose from a recognised medical condition — and then to consider whether or not the third test — causing substantial impairment of the defendant's ability to understand the nature of his or her conduct, or to form a rational judgement, or to exercise self-control — is satisfied. An example could be depression which gives rise to bouts of severe rage — here it could be argued that this could have substantially impaired the defendant's ability to exercise self-control.

Examiner tip
Do not refer to this defence except in murder cases, where the possibility of insanity could also be considered. For any offence other than murder, if there is any issue concerning any 'abnormality of mind', this can only be dealt with under insanity.

Loss of self-control

This defence replaces the defence of provocation. It is defined in ss. 54–56 of the **Coroners and Justice Act 2009**, which came into effect in October 2010.

As in the former law on provocation, the first requirement is for the defendant to prove that 'the killing must have resulted from the loss of self control'. The loss of control need not be sudden, but control must have been lost. Any time lapse, however, between the loss of self-control and the killing will have an effect on whether or not the jury accepts that the defendant had indeed lost his or her self-control at the time of the killing.

Before reaching the second requirement, the qualifying trigger, there is a further hurdle — that the defendant must not have been acting in a 'considered' desire for revenge. In the broad context of the legislative structure, there does not appear to be very much room for any 'considered' deliberation. 'In reality, the greater the level of deliberation, the less likely it will be that the killing followed a true loss of self control' — Lord Judge CJ in *R v Clinton* (2012). In *R v Ibrams and Gregory* (1981) the defence of provocation was disallowed on this ground and the same decision would be made here with loss of control.

The defendant then has to prove that this loss of control arose from a qualifying trigger — either it was 'attributable to D's fear of serious violence from V against D or another identified person' or it was 'attributable to a thing or things done or said (or both) which — (a) constituted circumstances of an extremely grave character, and (b) caused D to have a justifiable sense of being seriously wronged'.

The final trigger is a combination of the 'fear' and 'anger' triggers.

Knowledge check 5
What are the qualifying triggers for loss of control?

The 'fear trigger'

The first key issue here is that, as with self-defence, this is a subjective test — the defendant does not need to prove that his or her fear was reasonable; the jury need only be convinced that the fear was genuine. However, the fear must be of serious violence.

Second, the fear of serious violence has to be related to violence against the defendant or another identified person. So, for example, the defendant could be afraid that the victim would use serious violence against a companion; fear that the victim might use serious violence against someone unknown to the defendant is not sufficient.

Self-defence and the fear trigger

The new defence of loss of control, where the trigger is fear of serious violence, will in some circumstances overlap with self-defence, and may also be used in cases where the defendant has used excessive force and has killed the victim. However, it must be stressed that this is a separate defence and not a sub-species of self-defence as this fear trigger is not expressed in the same terms as self-defence.

This is arguably the position if the defendant has used force in anticipation of serious violence being used against him or her at some future time. In such cases, there are obvious difficulties in proving that there was a sufficient 'loss of self-control' and it may also be difficult to deny that there was a 'considered desire for revenge'.

In a case of reactive force, it is more likely that there will be evidence that the defendant lost self-control, and less likely that the defendant acted out of a considered desire for revenge.

Examiner tip

In any murder question where the loss of self-control defence is available through the fear trigger, consider also whether self-defence may be included.

The 'anger trigger'

Under s.55(3), the language used is quite emphatic. It is not enough that the defendant is fearful of violence. He must fear *serious* violence. In subsection (4)(a) the circumstances must not merely be grave, but *extremely* so. In subsection (4)(b) it is not enough that the defendant has been caused by the circumstances to feel a sense of grievance. It must arise from a *justifiable* sense not merely that he has been wronged, but that he has been '*seriously* wronged' — Lord Judge in *R* v *Clinton* (2012).

This means that the defendant him or herself must have a sense of having been seriously wronged in circumstances which he or she personally regarded as extremely grave, but this is not enough in itself — both the questions whether the circumstances were extremely grave, and whether the defendant's sense of grievance was justifiable require *objective* evaluation. It is clear that this provision raises the bar and makes it significantly more difficult to establish loss of control than the former defence of provocation.

Knowledge check 6

Why does the new loss of control 'anger' trigger raise the bar compared to the former defence of provocation?

'Fear and anger triggers' combined

The third qualifying trigger is where the defendant seeks to rely on both a fear of serious violence and a thing done or said. This could be relevant in cases where a person with the defendant's characteristics, and in his circumstances, would not have acted in the same way, as a result of the fear of serious violence alone or as a result of the thing(s) done or said alone, but he or she might have reacted in the same way as a result of *both* factors.

Issue of sexual fidelity

Under section 55 (6)(c) 'the fact that a thing done or said constituted sexual infidelity is to be disregarded'. Per explanatory notes:

> So, if a thing done or said, as referred to in section 55(4), amounts to sexual infidelity, that fact is disregarded in determining whether the qualifying trigger in section 55(4) applies. The effect is that, if a person kills another because they have been unfaithful, he or she will not be able to claim the partial defence. It is the fact of sexual infidelity that falls to be disregarded under the provision, so the thing done or said can still potentially amount to a qualifying trigger if (ignoring the sexual infidelity) it amounts nonetheless to circumstances of an extremely grave character causing the defendant to have a justifiable sense of being seriously wronged. This may arise only rarely, but an example of where it might be relevant is where a person discovers their partner sexually abusing their young child (an act that amounts to sexual infidelity) and loses self-control and kills. The fact that the partner's act amounted to sexual infidelity must be discounted but that act may still potentially be claimed to amount to the qualifying trigger in section 55(4) on the basis of the other aspects of the case (namely the child abuse).

This section unsurprisingly was the first to lead to an appeal being taken to the Court of Appeal — *R* v *Clinton* (2012). The appellant and his wife were undergoing a crisis in their marriage; there were financial problems and the defendant was also clinically depressed. Two weeks before her death, Mrs Clinton left for a trial separation but she would return to the family home to look after their children on their return from school until the appellant returned home. On the day before her death, she told her husband she was having an affair. That evening, her Land Rover was stolen and destroyed by her husband. The following day, he accessed the Facebook page of his wife and her lover and discovered graphic photographs and messages containing sexual innuendos. Having received a phone call from his wife, he confronted her at the family home, at which time he beat her and then strangled her to death.

The trial judge ruled that there was no evidence that the loss of self-control necessary for the purposes of this defence was due to one of the qualifying triggers identified in the statute, as she was required 'specifically' to disregard anything said or done that constituted sexual infidelity. The remarks allegedly made by the wife, challenged about her infidelity, to the effect that she had intercourse with five men were to be ignored. Such other evidence, she concluded, failed to meet the test of constituting circumstances which were of an extremely grave character or that they would cause the defendant to have a justifiable sense of being 'seriously wronged'. Accordingly, she withdrew the loss of control defence from the jury, leaving the defence of diminished responsibility, which the jury rejected.

In his decision to quash the conviction and order a retrial, Lord Judge CJ concluded that if sexual infidelity is the *only* element relied on to support a qualifying trigger, it has to be disregarded, but that it would be unrealistic to exclude such a consideration where it is 'integral' to the facts of the case. He stated:

Examiner tip

In any problem-solving question involving the issue of sexual infidelity, you will be expected to know the judgement given in *Clinton*.

...we do not see how any sensible evaluation of the gravity of the circumstances or their impact on the defendant could be made if the jury, having, in accordance with the legislation, heard the evidence, were then to be directed to excise from their evaluation of the qualifying trigger the matters said to constitute sexual infidelity, and to put them into distinct compartments to be disregarded. *In our judgement, where sexual infidelity is integral to and forms an essential part of the context in which to make a just evaluation whether a qualifying trigger properly falls within the ambit of subsections 55(3) and (4), the prohibition in section 55(6)(c) does not operate to exclude it.*

The objective test s.54 (1)(c)

The jury finally has to decide whether 'a person of D's sex and age, with a normal degree of tolerance and self-restraint and in the circumstances of D, might have reacted in the same or in a similar way to D'.

The most important change is in clarifying the 'reasonable man' test which has caused so much difficulty for courts, as shown by the conflicting judgements in *R* v *Smith* (Morgan James, 2000) and *Attorney-General of Jersey* v *Holley* (2005). This test no longer refers to the 'reasonable man' but, rather, to a person of normal degree of tolerance and self-restraint. The new rules also require that such a person 'might have reacted in the same or in a similar way to D' — it seems likely that at the least this will involve considering that such a person might have lost self-control *and* killed the victim.

It seems clear that the Act adopts the test from *Holley* (which largely re-stated the *Camplin* test) which provided for two separate tests to be considered by the jury — first, assessment of the gravity of the provocation which compels the jury to examine the actual circumstances of the loss of control and the question of the 'qualifying trigger', and then the second test which is a wholly objective one (apart from the jury being able to take into account the defendant's age and gender). However, the new law contains the additional words 'and in the circumstances of D', although this phrase is qualified by providing that it excludes circumstances 'whose only relevance to D's conduct is that they bear on D's general capacity for tolerance or self-restraint'. It can be argued — in the absence of new case law — that these words mean that the old *Camplin* ruling may be followed — and even that 'repugnant characteristics' from *Morhall* may be included — provided that they are the focus of the qualifying trigger. Therefore, a defendant's history of abuse at the hands of the victim could be taken into account in deciding whether an ordinary person might have acted as the defendant did, whereas the defendant's generally short temper could not.

It is also clear that alcoholism, for example, or another mental deficiency or disorder that is liable to affect temper and tolerance must be excluded. A person who has killed because his or her capacity for self-control was reduced by such a characteristic must look to the defence of diminished responsibility for a partial defence as decided in *Holley* because such characteristics constitute an abnormality of mental functioning, unlike, for example, the defendant's age.

Abnormal states of mind, such as intoxication or irritability, should also be left out, as should other factors that affect a general capacity to exercise adequate self-control, like a claim that the defendant is 'more jealous or obsessive than most'. The ruling in *R* v *Newell* will stand.

Knowledge check 7

What is the objective test for loss of self-control?

Involuntary manslaughter

Involuntary manslaughter includes all types of homicide (unlawful killing) committed *without* malice aforethought (specific intention to kill or commit GBH). It has always been the most difficult of homicides to construe because its *mens rea* is defined in the negative. It has been observed by Lord Atkin that:

> ...of all crimes, manslaughter appears to afford most difficulties of definition, for it concerns homicide in so many and so varying conditions...the law...recognises murder on the one hand based mainly, though not exclusively, on an intention to kill, and manslaughter on the other hand, based mainly, though not exclusively, on the absence of intent to kill, but with the presence of an element of 'unlawfulness' which is the elusive factor.

A further source of difficulty is that, in a sense, manslaughter is caught between murder at the extreme end of criminal liability and accidental death at the other end, where no criminal liability usually attaches.

Currently, the law recognises three broad categories of involuntary manslaughter:
- manslaughter by an unlawful and dangerous act
- manslaughter by gross negligence
- reckless manslaughter

Manslaughter by unlawful and dangerous act

According to Smith and Hogan in *Criminal Law*:

> A defendant is guilty of manslaughter if he kills by an unlawful and dangerous act. The only *mens rea* required is an intention to do that act and any fault required to render it unlawful. It is irrelevant that the defendant is unaware that it is unlawful or that it is dangerous, and that he is unaware of the circumstances which make it dangerous, if a reasonable person would have been aware of them.

Unlawful act

It is now established that for an act to be unlawful for the purposes of this offence, it must be a crime. A tort or breach of contract is not enough. In *R v Franklin* (1883), which involved the tort of trespass, the trial judge ruled: 'The mere fact of a civil wrong committed by one person against another ought not to be used as an incident which is a necessary step in a criminal case.' It seems to be settled law from the cases of *R v Lamb* (1967) and *R v Jennings* (1990) that a criminal act must be identified and proved, including the necessary *mens rea*. It was because no initial crime was proved to have been committed that Lamb's conviction was quashed on appeal. This was also the case in *R v Scarlett* (1993), where the defendant's conviction was quashed because the Crown had not been able to produce evidence that the defendant's use of force had been unreasonable and was therefore unlawful.

It is vital to understand that the *mens rea* for involuntary manslaughter is that of the initial crime — and it can be intention or recklessness. Although most cases involve some form of assault, which requires intention or subjective recklessness, in *DPP v Newbury and Jones* (1976), the initial offence (which was not identified in the case) was surely that of criminal damage, for which objective recklessness was

Knowledge check 8

What are the three types of involuntary manslaughter?

required (see *MPC* v *Caldwell* 1982). However, the case of *R* v *G* (2003) has since abolished the requirement of objective recklessness in cases of criminal damage. As regards omission, it seems to be the case, following *R* v *Lowe* (1973), that if the omission is no more than an act of negligence, this will not be the basis of manslaughter by unlawful dangerous act unless the omission is truly wilful, for example a deliberate omission to summon emergency medical aid, knowing it to be necessary. Omissions that cause death should therefore be dealt with under the law on manslaughter by gross negligence.

Knowledge check 9

Which case confirms that the unlawful act must be a crime?

Dangerous act

In *R* v *Church* (1966), Edmund-Davies J stated:

> For such a verdict to follow, the unlawful act must be such as all sober and reasonable people would inevitably recognise must subject the other person to, at least, the risk of some harm resulting therefrom, albeit not serious harm.

The test of dangerousness is therefore objective. The question is further extended to consider whether the reasonable person would have appreciated that the act was dangerous in the light not only of the circumstances actually known to the defendant, but also of any additional circumstances of which the hypothetical person would have been aware; see the leading case of *R* v *Watson* (1989), but note that the defendant's conviction for the manslaughter during a burglary of an 87-year-old man was overturned on appeal on the ground that causation had not been proved.

Knowledge check 10

What is the test to establish whether or not the unlawful act was also dangerous?

In *R* v *Dawson* (1985), where an armed robbery at a petrol station had led to the station attendant's death from a heart attack, the original conviction for manslaughter was quashed on appeal because, it seems, the court assumed that in the context of this offence, 'harm' includes 'injury to the person through the operation of shock emanating from fright'. As Professor J. C. Smith comments in *Criminal Law*: 'It seems that it is not enough that the act is likely to frighten. It must be likely to cause such shock as to result in physical injury.'

Causation

The unlawful and dangerous act must be the cause of the victim's death. At one time, it was considered that the act had to be directed at the victim, but following *R* v *Goodfellow* (1986), it is now clear that if the act satisfies both the normal factual and legal rules of causation, this will suffice for such a charge to be brought.

Manslaughter by gross negligence

Manslaughter by gross negligence is based on the civil tort of negligence and is most commonly the result of an omission — a failure to act where there is a clear duty to act (see *R* v *Stone and Dobinson*, 1977). The view of Lord Hewart CJ in *R* v *Bateman* (1925) is still important:

> In order to establish criminal liability, the facts must be such that in the opinion of the jury, the negligence of the accused went beyond a mere matter of compensation between subjects (civil tort liability) and showed such disregard for the life and safety of others as to amount to a crime against the state and conduct deserving punishment.

Duty of care

To obtain a conviction for manslaughter by gross negligence, the Crown must show that there is a duty of care owed by the defendant to the victim. This issue has caused considerable difficulty but, following *R* v *Adomako* (1994), it now appears that the duty of care is simply based on the 'neighbour' test in *Donoghue* v *Stevenson* (1932) or on the incremental approach in *Caparo Industries plc* v *Dickman* (1990). For both cases, see *Student Unit Guide AQA A2 Unit 4, Criminal Law (Offences Against Property) and Tort Law*, in this series. The test is therefore whether it was reasonably foreseeable that the victim would be injured.

Note, however, that a duty of care can also be established by using the rules on omission in *actus reus,* e.g. assumption of a voluntary duty (e.g. *R* v *Stone and Dobinson*, 1977) and creating a dangerous situation (e.g. *R* v *Miller*, 1983).

However, the more recent case of *R* v *Singh* (1999) established the current rule whereby 'the circumstances must be such that a reasonably prudent person would have foreseen a serious and obvious risk not merely of injury or even of serious injury but of death'. In *R* v *Misra and Srivastava* (2004), two doctors were convicted of gross negligence manslaughter after a patient died from toxic-shock syndrome (where a simple course of antibiotics would have saved his life), and the Court of Appeal confirmed this test — that the risk to which the victim must be exposed is a risk of death. In *Brown* v *R* (2005), the Privy Council even suggested that only a very high risk of death would suffice.

Breach of duty of care

The test for what constitutes a breach of the duty of care causing the death of the victim is again the tort test. The defendant's conduct must have gone below the standard to be expected of a reasonable person. This then requires the various 'risk' factors to be considered, for example probability of harm and seriousness of injury. Note the second part of the rule for gross negligence manslaughter, that the breach must have caused death. To judge whether it has done so, the legal rules of causation need to be considered, and also the factual 'but for' test, where the question is asked: but for the defendant's action, would the defendant still be alive?

Gross negligence

Gross negligence is the *mens rea* for the offence and, as can be seen from Lord Hewart CJ's statement in *R* v *Bateman* (above), this is a question for the jury to decide. It must consider whether, having regard to the risk of death involved, the conduct of the defendant was so bad in all the circumstances as to amount in its judgement to a criminal act or omission.

In *R* v *Adomako*, Lord Taylor CJ indicated that gross negligence could include the following:
- indifference to an obvious risk of injury to health
- actual foresight of the risk, coupled with the determination nevertheless to run it
- an appreciation of the risk, coupled with an intention to avoid it but also coupled with such a high degree of negligence in the attempted avoidance as the jury considers conviction justified

Examiner tip
If the scenario facts support this, it is much easier to argue that a duty of care arises from one of criminal omissions, than to analyse either the neighbour test from *Donoghue* v *Stevenson* or the incremental approach from *Caparo*.

Knowledge check 11
Which case established the rule that there must be a risk of death?

Examiner tip

The most commonly used of these four examples is inattention or failure to address a serious risk (of death) that went beyond carelessness in respect of an obvious and important matter that the defendant's duty demanded he should address.

- inattention or failure to address a serious risk that went beyond 'mere inadvertence' in respect of an obvious and important matter that the defendant's duty demanded he should address

In this case, the defendant was an anaesthetist who, during an eye operation, failed to notice that the patient's breathing tube had become disconnected. In the 4 minutes between the disconnection and the alarm sounding on the machine monitoring the patient's blood pressure, the defendant also failed to notice that the patient was turning blue through anoxia, the dials on the ventilating machine were not operating and the alarm on the ventilator was not switched on. An expert witness stated that these problems would have been obvious to any competent anaesthetist within 15 seconds. The case was appealed to the House of Lords, with the result that this branch of the law returned to the traditional rules laid down in *R* v *Bateman* and *Andrews* v *DPP* (1937).

Summary

Murder

Unlawful killing with intention either to kill or commit grievous bodily harm. Note both direct and oblique intent cases.

Voluntary manslaughter

- Diminished responsibility (amended) s.2 of the Homicide Act 1957.
- Loss of self-control: this defence replaces the defence of provocation — ss. 54–56 of the **Coroners and Justice Act 2009**. As in the former law on provocation, the first requirement is for the defendant to prove that 'the killing must have resulted from the loss of self-control'. This need not be sudden and the defendant must not have been acting in a 'considered' desire for revenge.
- Loss of control must arise from a qualifying trigger — either it was 'attributable to D's fear of serious violence from V against D or another identified person' or it was 'attributable to a thing or things done or said (or both) which (a) constituted circumstances of an extremely grave character, (b) caused D to have a justifiable sense of being seriously wronged'.
- Note 'the fact that a thing done or said constituted sexual infidelity is to be disregarded', but see *R* v *Clinton*.

- The final trigger is a combination of the 'fear' and 'anger' triggers.
- Objective test: the jury finally has to decide whether 'a person of D's sex and age, with a normal degree of tolerance and self-restraint and in the circumstances of D, might have reacted in the same or in a similar way to D'.

Involuntary manslaughter

This is unlawful killing without malice aforethought.
- Unlawful dangerous act manslaughter:
  - unlawful act must be a crime
  - must be objectively dangerous 'as to some harm'
  - must be the cause of death
- Gross negligence manslaughter:
  - based on civil tort of negligence — duty of care: neighbour test or *Caparo* incremental approach, but also *actus reus* omissions, e.g. creating a dangerous situation
  - must be a serious and obvious risk of death
  - breach of duty of care — 'reasonable man' test
  - causation and remoteness tests from negligence
- Gross negligence: the jury must consider whether, having regard to the risk of death involved, the conduct of the defendant was so bad in all the circumstances as to amount in its judgement to a criminal act or omission.

Defences

In this unit, students are usually required to consider defences that may be available to the defendant, in addition to explaining the *actus reus* and *mens rea* of the appropriate offence.

Consent

Like the defence of intoxication, consent has limited and controlled applications. Indeed, the general rule is that it is *not* a defence where non-fatal crimes are concerned. In *Attorney General's Reference (No. 6 of 1980)*, the Court of Appeal decided that where two people fight, the blows inflicted can amount to battery, and that the unlawfulness cannot be denied by one party pleading that the other consented to the fight.

This confirms the view taken by Swift J in *R v Donovan* (1934), where he stated: 'It is an unlawful act to beat another person with such a degree of violence that the infliction of bodily harm is a probable consequence, and when such an act is proved, consent is immaterial.'

The first rule to be established if consent is to be pleaded successfully is that the alleged victim's consent must not have been obtained by deception or, if it was, then the deception must not have been such as to alter his or her perception of the nature and quality of the act complained of. In *R v Richardson* (1999), the defendant was a registered dentist who had been suspended from practice by the General Dental Council. While suspended, she had carried out dentistry on a number of patients, and the mother of two of these patients complained to the police. A prosecution was brought for actual bodily harm (ABH) and the defendant was convicted. On appeal she argued that the complainant had consented to the treatment. The appeal was allowed because there had been no deception as to the nature and quality of the dental work; if there had been, it would have cancelled out the consent.

A potentially broader interpretation of this question of consent was taken in *R v Tabassum* (2000), where it was held that a mistake as to the medical qualifications of the defendant meant that the victim did not know the quality of the act the defendant carried out and therefore could not have consented to it.

The next general rule is that consent may only be pleaded to the crimes of assault and battery and not to any more serious crime, unless the circumstances fall under the following heads:

● Sporting activities such as football, rugby and hockey, where physical contact is effectively part of the sport. In these cases, players are deemed to have consented to even serious injuries, provided these occurred when the players were acting within the rules of the game; see *R v Billinghurst* (1978). However, in *R v Barnes* (2004), Lord Woolf CJ ruled that:

> ...In highly competitive sports, where conduct outside the rules could be expected to occur in the heat of the moment, such conduct might not reach the threshold level required for it to be criminal. That level was an objective one which would be determined by the type of sport, the level at which it was played...the degree of force used, the extent of the risk of injury and the state of mind of the accused.

Examiner tip
When dealing with the defence of consent, consider (a) whether or not the consent was genuine and valid; then (b) whether the circumstances come within the exceptions to the general rule, such as rough horseplay or surgery.

Knowledge check 12
Why was it decided in *Richardson* that consent was validly given but not in *Tabassum*?

Knowledge check 13
What change in the law on organised sports was made in the case of *R v Barnes*?

- Rough horseplay. In *R* v *Jones* (1987), a gang of schoolboys threw their victims up to 3 metres into the air, with the result that one victim suffered a ruptured spleen and broke his arm on hitting the floor. The defence was allowed on the basis that there was no intention to cause injury, and on appeal, convictions for grievous bodily harm (GBH) were quashed. Another case to illustrate this exception is *R* v *Richardson and Irwin* (1999). The defendants, who were intoxicated, indulged in horseplay in which the victim was held over a balcony: he fell and suffered serious injuries and the defendants were convicted of a s.20 GBH offence. Having quashed their convictions, the court held that, where a defendant pleads voluntary intoxication in response to an offence of basic intent, the Crown must prove that the defendant would have foreseen the risk, had he or she not been intoxicated. It was also held that a mistaken belief by a defendant that his or her victim was consenting to run the risk of personal injury would enable the defendant to avoid liability, even if that mistake was induced by intoxication.

- Surgery, including tattooing and body piercing. In *R* v *Wilson* (1996), the defendant had, at his wife's request, used a hot knife to brand his initials onto her bottom. The scars were found during a medical examination and he was subsequently charged with s.47 ABH. At his trial, it was argued that his wife had consented to his conduct, but the judge ruled (following *R* v *Brown,* a 1994 case involving sadomasochism) that this defence was not available on these facts. However, his appeal was allowed on the basis that it fell within the exception of tattooing recognised by *R* v *Brown,* from which case it was distinguished on the ground that Mrs Wilson had not only consented to the branding but had actually instigated it, and there was clearly no aggressive intent on the part of the husband.

Examiner tip

When dealing with the defence of consent, consider whether in the circumstances, consent may *initially* have been given but then *withdrawn* prior to the actions of the defendant which actually caused the injury, e.g. two teenage boys consent to a 'mock' wrestling contest, but after one boy has indicated that he 'concedes', the other breaks his arm in a wrestling hold.

Insanity

The legal rules governing decisions about the criminal liability of insane people are known as the **M'Naghten rules**. These state that:

> To establish a defence on the ground of insanity, it must be clearly proved that, at the time of the committing of the act, the party accused was labouring under such a defect of reason, from disease of the mind, as not to know the nature and quality of the act he was doing, or, if he did know it, that he did not know he was doing what was wrong.

As with the partial defence of diminished responsibility, the burden of proof rests on the defendant and the standard of proof is the balance of probability.

To sum up, a defendant must be acquitted:
- if, because of a disease of the mind, he or she did not know the nature and quality of his or her act
- if, because of a disease of the mind, he or she did not know his or her act was wrong, even if he or she did know the nature and quality of his or her act

After the introduction of the partial defence of diminished responsibility under s.2 of the **Homicide Act 1957**, this defence was rarely used. However, in the 5 years since the introduction of the **Criminal Procedure (Insanity) Act 1991**, there were 44 findings of 'not guilty by reason of insanity'.

Knowledge check 14

What are the M'Naghten rules?

Smith and Hogan Criminal Law states:

> When a defendant puts his state of mind in issue, the question of whether he has raised the defence of insanity is one of law for the judge. Whether a defendant, or indeed his medical witnesses, would call the condition on which he relies 'insanity' is immaterial. The expert witnesses may testify as to the factual nature of the condition but it is for the judge to say whether that is evidence of a 'defect of reason from disease of the mind' because these are legal, not medical concepts.

Disease of the mind

Any disease that produces a mental malfunctioning is a disease of the mind. Physical conditions such as arteriosclerosis, brain tumours, epilepsy and diabetes may all amount in law to diseases of the mind if they produce the relevant malfunction. A malfunctioning of the mind is *not* a disease of the mind when it is brought about by some external factor, for example a blow on the head causing concussion or the consumption of alcohol or drugs. In *Bratty* v *Attorney General for Northern Ireland* (1963), Lord Denning MR defined a disease of the mind as follows: 'It seems to me that any mental disorder which has manifested itself in violence and is prone to recur is a disease of the mind.'

In *R* v *Kemp* (1957), the defendant, who was suffering from arteriosclerosis, made a savage attack on his wife with a hammer. It was argued that his defect of reason arose from a purely physical condition and not from any mental disease. Devlin J rejected this argument and ruled that the defendant was suffering from a disease of the mind, stating 'in my judgement the condition of the brain is irrelevant and so is the question of whether the condition of the mind is curable or incurable, transitory or permanent.'

Knowledge check 15

How did Lord Denning define disease of the mind in *Bratty*?

Defect of reason

The basis of the M'Naghten rules is that the disease of the mind must have given rise to a defect of reason. This means that the defendant's powers of reasoning must have been impaired; a mere failure to use the powers of reasoning that one has is not within the rules. See *R* v *Clarke* (1972), where the defendant claimed she had taken articles from a supermarket without paying for them because of absentmindedness resulting from depression. It was held that, even if she was suffering from a disease of the mind, she had not raised the defence of insanity but was simply denying that she had *mens rea*.

Not knowing the nature and quality of the act

The ignorance referred to here is ignorance of the physical, rather than the moral, nature of the act, for example where a man cuts a woman's throat, believing he is cutting a loaf of bread, or where a nurse throws a baby into a fire thinking it is a log. People who kill under the influence of delusions such as these cannot be convicted of murder as they lack the required *mens rea*.

Not knowing the act is wrong

It is established law that this requirement means legally and not morally wrong. Even if the defendant did not know that his or her action was against the law, he or she is still liable if he or she knew it was wrong 'according to the ordinary standard adopted by reasonable men'.

Knowledge check 16

Why was Windle's defence of insanity rejected by the trial judge?

Examiner tip

Generally, for murder questions, if the defendant is suffering from some mental condition, it is better to consider this under diminished responsibility rather than insanity. However, if time permits, you could add a brief paragraph dealing with the M'Naghten rules. For all crimes other than murder, any indication that the defendant is suffering from any mental condition can *only* be dealt with under insanity.

In *R* v *Windle* (1952), the defendant killed his wife, who was certifiably insane and always speaking of committing suicide. He then telephoned the police and, when he was arrested, said: 'I suppose they will hang me for this.' At his trial, the defence of insanity was not allowed to go to the jury, since the words he used indicated that he knew killing his wife was legally wrong.

Automatism

Automatism is recognised as a defence to all crimes. It refers to the situation where the defendant's actions are involuntary, in the sense that they are beyond his or her control. Typical examples are reflex actions and acts committed while sleepwalking or undergoing a hypnotic trance or convulsions.

The rationale for this defence is clear. The defendant in such a situation is not responsible for the consequences of his or her actions. The act is, in a sense, not his or her own. He or she does not deserve to be punished, nor would punishment serve any useful or rational purpose.

Although automatism has been referred to as a 'defence', the legally accurate analysis is that voluntariness is a basic ingredient of criminal liability. The onus, therefore, is on the prosecution to prove beyond reasonable doubt that the conduct of the defendant was willed.

Lord Denning MR in *Bratty* v *Attorney General for Northern Ireland* stated:

> The requirement that it should be a voluntary act is essential...in every criminal case. No act is punishable if it is done involuntarily; and an involuntary act in this context — some people...prefer to speak of it as 'automatism' — means an act which is done by the muscles without any control by the mind, such as a spasm, a reflex action or a convulsion; or an act done by a person who is not conscious of what he is doing, such as an act done whilst suffering from concussion or whilst sleepwalking.

He went on to stress that an act is not to be regarded as involuntary if the person was conscious but nevertheless could not control his or her actions (irresistible impulse) or could not remember after the event exactly what took place.

In *Broome* v *Perkins* (1987), the defendant was charged with driving without due care and attention. He had driven erratically for 6 miles. It was held that even though there was some evidence to establish that he was suffering from hypoglycaemia (low blood sugar), he must have been exercising conscious control of the vehicle, even though imperfectly, in order to have manoeuvred it reasonably successfully over such a distance.

Insane automatism

If the automatism results from a 'disease of the mind' under the M'Naghten rules, the condition amounts to what in law is known as insanity. In such circumstances, the defendant is entitled to no more than a qualified acquittal by the special verdict of 'not guilty by reason of insanity'. In such a case, the judge must make one of various orders under the **Criminal Procedure (Insanity and Unfitness to Plead) Act 1991**.

For a defendant to have what amounts to a 'disease of the mind', it does not matter whether the cause of the mental impairment is organic (as in epilepsy) or functional (as in schizophrenia). Nor does it matter whether the impairment is permanent or transient and intermittent, provided that it was operative at the time of the alleged offence (see the 1984 case of *R* v *Sullivan*). In *Bratty*, Lord Denning MR said that any condition that has 'manifested itself in violence and is prone to recur is a disease of the mind'.

Non-insane automatism

This defence may apply where the automatism is induced by an external factor such as a blow to the head causing concussion or a reflex spasm. This gives rise to criticism when acts committed by someone sleepwalking or undergoing an epileptic episode fall to be considered as acts of insane automatism. The law on automatism as it affects diabetics has been the subject of particular criticism because, depending on whether the diabetic's diagnosis is hypoglycaemia (low blood sugar) or hyperglycaemia (high blood sugar), the appropriate defence is judged to be non-insane or insane automatism respectively. In *R* v *Quick* (1973), a defendant who took his insulin but failed to eat was able to plead non-insane automatism, but in *R* v *Hennessy* (1989), a defendant who had failed to take sufficient insulin was held to have a defence of insane automatism (which, incidentally, caused him to change his plea to guilty rather than face indefinite detention in a mental hospital).

In *R* v *T* (1990), the application of the internal/external factor test led to a just decision. The defendant, who suffered from post-traumatic stress disorder as a consequence of being raped, stabbed someone during a robbery. The trial judge ruled that the stress had been caused by the external factor of the rape and accordingly the defence was that of non-insane automatism. Note that where a defendant's automatism has been caused by the consumption of alcohol or dangerous drugs, the defence becomes intoxication.

Knowledge check 17

Why was it decided in *Hennessy* that the defence was one of insane automatism?

Self-defence

Where an attack of a violent, unlawful or indecent nature is made so that the victim fears for his or her life or safety, then he or she is entitled to protect himself or herself and to repel such attack by force, provided that he or she uses no more force than is reasonable in the circumstances; see Lord Morris's comments in *Palmer* v *R* (1971).

There is a common law right of self-defence. In addition, s.3(1) of the **Criminal Law Act 1967** states: 'A person may use such force as is reasonable in the circumstances in the prevention of crime, or in effecting or assisting in the lawful arrest of offenders or suspected offenders or of persons unlawfully at large.' Where justified, self-defence can provide a complete defence to charges of murder or any non-fatal offence against the person; the defence operates by negating the unlawfulness of the homicide or assault. Section 76 of the **Criminal Justice and Immigration Act 2008** clarifies the operation of both the common law and statutory rules.

The first requirement (as stated by Janet Loveless in *Complete Criminal Law: Test, Cases, and Materials*) is that 'defensive force will only be lawful if it is necessary, and it will only be necessary if it is used to resist, repel or ward off an unjust imminent threat. The act of self-defence cannot be retaliatory or revengeful'. An attack at some future point will not be sufficiently imminent — this means 'fairly immediate'.

The second requirement is that the degree of force must be reasonable. Factors that may be taken into account in determining what is reasonable force for the purpose of both common-law and statutory defences are:

- the nature and degree of force used
- the gravity of the crime or evil to be prevented
- the relative strength of the parties concerned and the number of people involved

The law does not require proportionate force, but the degree of force must be capable of being seen as only so much as is necessary to repel an attack. The 2008 Act states that 'a person acting for a legitimate purpose may not be able to weigh to a nicety the exact measure of any necessary action'. Excessive force will usually be evidence that the attack was retaliatory and therefore not in self-defence; see *R* v *Martin* (2002).

To reject self-defence as a defence, the jury must be satisfied that no reasonable person, put in the defendant's position and with the time for reflection that the defendant had, would consider the violence he or she used to be justifiable; see *Farrell* v *Secretary of State for Defence* (1980). Thus, objectivity is tempered with the personal situation of the actual defendant. The test is whether or not the defendant used reasonable force in the agony of the situation, and not whether the force used would be considered reasonable by the defendant or a reasonable person, viewing the situation in cool isolation. In *R* v *Owino* (1995) it was confirmed that this test combines both subjective and objective elements.

Knowledge check 18

What are the two tests for self-defence?

Further points to consider

- Where the defendant has used excessive (and therefore unreasonable) force, neither the common law nor the statutory defence of self-defence will be open to him or her, and his or her criminal liability will be determined by his or her *mens rea* and the harm he or she has inflicted.
- The law has no sympathy with drunkenness, so that an honest mistake made by a drunken defendant will render the defence of self-defence inadmissible; see *R* v *O'Grady* (1987).
- As to the duty of a defendant to retreat before acting in self-defence, the case of *R* v *Bird* (1985) held that proof that the defendant in this case had tried to retreat was a method of rebutting the suggestion that she was an attacker, but was not the only method.
- It also appears from *Attorney General's Reference (No. 2 of 1983)* that, in certain circumstances, a person is not obliged to wait until he or she is attacked before taking steps towards self-protection. This was also confirmed in *R* v *Beckford* (1988) where it was held that circumstances could justify a pre-emptive strike.
- The lawful use of self-defence is limited when it comes to protecting property.

Mistake

In cases where defendants have defended themselves because they honestly but mistakenly believed themselves to be under attack, the defence of self-defence must be judged according to the mistaken view of the facts, regardless of whether the mistake was reasonable or not. In *R* v *Williams* (1984), where the defendant punched the victim in the (mistaken) belief that he was trying to rescue another from being unlawfully attacked, he was convicted of ABH under s.47, following a direction to the jury that his mistake would be relevant only if it was honest and based on reasonable grounds.

On appeal it was held that in such cases the defendant had to be judged according to his mistaken view of the facts, even if that belief was unreasonable.

Intoxication

Students often find the defence of intoxication difficult to deal with because the way in which it operates, if at all, depends on variables in terms of types of intoxication — whether voluntary or involuntary, whether by alcohol or illegal drugs or by sedative or prescribed drugs — and on whether or not the particular offence charged is an offence of basic or specific intent.

The first general rule to learn is that, as *Smith and Hogan Criminal Law* states:

> Intoxication is not, and never has been, a defence in itself. It is never a defence for a defendant to say, however convincingly, that but for the drink he would not have behaved as he did. Because alcohol and other drugs weaken the restraints and inhibitions which normally govern our conduct, a man may do things when drunk that he would never dream of doing while sober. If, however, he had the *mens rea* for the crime charged he is guilty, even though drink impaired or negatived his ability to judge between right and wrong or to resist temptation or provocation and even though, in his drunken state, he found the impulse to act as he did irresistible.

Voluntary intoxication by alcohol or illegal drugs

The legal rule is that voluntary intoxication by alcohol or illegal drugs is at best a partial defence for anyone charged with offences of specific intent such as murder and s.18 GBH with intent. For basic intent offences, it will be rejected. In the leading case of *DPP* v *Beard* (1920), it was held that if a defendant charged with murder can prove that, at the time of committing the crime, he or she was so drunk as to be unable to form the necessary *mens rea* of intent for the crime, he or she will be acquitted of that offence but convicted of the basic-intent offence — so that the verdict will not be murder but manslaughter, and, in other cases, not s.18 GBH but s.20. However, the courts have relaxed this rule somewhat, on the basis that it would not be fair to require the defendant to prove his or her incapacity. The test now is whether the defendant's intoxication negated his or her specific intent because it prevented him or her from foreseeing the prohibited consequence. In *DPP* v *Majewski* (1977), this approach was confirmed. Here the defendant was charged with the assault of a policeman — an offence of basic intent — and his defence of drunkenness was rejected.

As for intoxication by illegal drugs, the same applies. In *R* v *Lipman* (1970), the defendant, having taken a quantity of LSD and believing as a result that he was being attacked by snakes in the centre of the earth, attacked and killed his girlfriend, cramming a sheet into her mouth. At his trial, he was acquitted of murder, but his plea of intoxication was not accepted as a defence to manslaughter. The Court of Appeal stated that when a killing results from an unlawful act of the defendant, no specific

Knowledge check 20

Which two cases confirm that voluntary intoxication, either by alcohol or by dangerous drugs, is not available for basic intent offences?

Examiner tip

Carefully read the scenario and decide which factors are relevant — whether intoxication, voluntary or involuntary, and the nature of the offence (specific or basic intent). Then explain and apply the appropriate legal rules.

intent has to be proved to convict of manslaughter. Self-induced intoxication is no defence, and since the acts complained of were obviously likely to harm the victim, the verdict of manslaughter was inevitable.

Voluntary intoxication using sedative drugs

If a defendant has taken drugs that normally have a sedative or soporific effect, making the user relaxed or sleepy, he or she is usually treated as being involuntarily intoxicated. In *R v Hardie* (1985), the defendant, after taking Valium tablets prescribed for the woman with whom he shared a flat, started a fire when she asked him to leave, and he was charged and convicted under the **Criminal Damage Act 1971**. The Court of Appeal, quashing this conviction, overturned the trial judge's direction to the jury, which had made no mention of the distinction the law draws between dangerous/illegal and prescription/sedative drugs. The court also indicated that, in this case, the jury should have been invited to consider whether the defendant's taking of six Valium tablets was objectively reckless; following *R v G* (2003), the test would now be one of subjective recklessness.

Involuntary intoxication

Involuntary intoxication refers to the situation where defendants claim that they did not know they were taking alcohol or an intoxicating drug because their food or drink was laced without their knowledge. The legal rule here is that, if this negates the *mens rea* of the offence, it will be a full defence to any type of offence, whether one of specific or basic intent.

However, in the difficult case of *R v Kingston* (1994), which involved a defendant who was attracted to young boys, the defendant was drugged without his knowledge by his co-defendant, who had intended to blackmail him. His defence to a charge of indecent assault was that the involuntary intoxication effectively disinhibited him, and that, if sober, he would not have carried out these acts. The Court of Appeal allowed his appeal, holding that if a surreptitiously administered drug causes a person to lose his self-control and so form an intent he would not otherwise have formed, the law should not hold him or her liable, as the operative fault is not his or hers. This novel argument was rejected by the House of Lords, which approved the trial judge's direction to the jury that an intoxicated intent was still intent, and the fact that the intoxication was involuntary made no difference.

Intoxication causing insanity or abnormality of mind

It is settled law that, where excessively heavy drinking causes actual insanity, such as the condition of *delirium tremens*, then the M'Naghten rules apply and the defence becomes one of insanity. As regards the issue of abnormality of mind giving rise to the possible (partial) defence to murder of diminished responsibility under s.2 of the **Homicide Act 1957**, it is also clear that self-induced intoxication must be ignored in deciding whether the defendant was suffering from such an abnormality of mind as to amount to diminished responsibility; exceptions to this arise if it can be proved that the defendant suffered from alcohol dependency syndrome, which caused an abnormality of mind, or that the craving for drink or drugs was itself an abnormality of mind; see *R v Wood* (2008) and *R v Dietschmann* (2003), pp. 13–14.

- **Consent.** General rule — only available for assault or battery unless the circumstances of the case fall into the recognised exceptions: organised sports, rough horseplay and surgery. Consent must be genuine — not obtained by deception.

- **Insanity.** M'Naghten rules — defendant must prove that, at the time of the committing of the act, he or she was labouring under such a defect of reason, from disease of the mind, as not to know the nature and quality of the act he or she was doing, or, if he or she did know it, that he or she did not know he or she was doing what was wrong.

- As with the partial defence of diminished responsibility, the burden of proof rests on the defendant and the standard of proof is the balance of probability.

- Any disease that produces a mental malfunctioning is a disease of the mind, including physical conditions such as arteriosclerosis, brain tumours, epilepsy and diabetes.

- **Automatism.** The defendant's actions are involuntary, in the sense that they are beyond his or her control. Typical examples are reflex actions and acts committed while sleepwalking or undergoing a hypnotic trance or convulsions. If caused by an internal factor, this will be insane automatism which is the same as insanity. If induced by an external factor, it will be non-insane automatism.

- **Self-defence.** Common law defence, but see also the **Criminal Law Act 1967** and the **Criminal Justice and Immigration Act 2008**:
  - use of force must be necessary and reasonable in the circumstances
  - test of reasonableness is both subjective and objective
  - defence is lost if excessive force is used
  - no need to retreat
  - pre-emptive force may be used

- **Mistake.** Mistaken belief must be honestly held — need not be reasonable.

- **Intoxication.** Rules depend on the following issues:
  - whether voluntary or involuntary
  - whether by alcohol/illegal drugs or by sedative or prescribed drugs
  - whether or not the particular offence charged is an offence of basic or specific intent

Critical evaluation of law on offences against the person and defences

In this examination paper, Question 3 is always about how well you can evaluate or criticise a particular area of law. Questions may be set on:

- non-fatal offences
- murder including loss of self-control and diminished responsibility
- general defences — the question will require the selection of **two** defences

The question may also require you to suggest and comment on possible reforms.

Critical evaluation of the law on non-fatal offences

Terminology

First, it may be said that the non-fatal offences are badly defined. There are still no clear statutory definitions of assault and battery, while the definitions of the more serious offences are contained in an Act passed well over 100 years ago. The Act has been described as 'a rag-bag of offences brought together from a wide variety of sources with no attempt, as the draftsman frankly acknowledged, to introduce consistency as to substance or as to form'. Much of the vocabulary, such as 'assault' in s.47 and 'maliciously' in s.18, is antiquated and even misleading. In s.18, the word 'maliciously' means nothing in its primary use because the *mens rea* is already defined as 'with intent', whereas in s.20 the same word means recklessness or basic intent as to inflicting some harm. The word 'wounding' again has a technical rather than common definition.

Another linguistic criticism concerns the use of 'inflict' in s.20 and 'cause' in s.18 of the **Offences Against the Person Act 1861**. It is argued that the word 'inflict' requires a battery to take place for the full offence to be committed, and this was the central issue raised in the case of *R* v *Burstow* (1997), decided by the House of Lords. The Court of Appeal in that case had certified the question: 'Whether an offence of inflicting grievous bodily harm under s.20 can be committed where no physical violence is applied directly or indirectly.' It was argued that it is inherent in the word 'inflict' that there must be some application of force to the body, but in the earlier case of *R* v *Wilson* (1984), Lord Roskill was 'content to accept that there can be the infliction of GBH contrary to s.20 without an assault (battery) being committed'. Lord Steyn, in the leading judgement in *R* v *Burstow*, ruled that 'there is no radical difference between the meaning of the words "cause" and "inflict"'. Lord Hope went even further when he stated that 'for all practical purposes there is, in my opinion, no difference between these two words'. In a later section he continued: 'In the context of a criminal act, therefore, the words "cause" and "inflict" may be taken to be interchangeable.'

Knowledge check 21

In which case was it decided that the words 'cause' and 'inflict' have the same meaning?

Students need to be aware of the secondary *mens rea* for a s.18 offence — 'intention to resist or prevent the lawful apprehension of any person'. Although it was stated in *R* v *Mowatt* (1968) that the word 'malicious' means nothing, *Smith and Hogan Criminal Law* submits that, as regards this particular section, the prosecution needs to be able to prove that a defendant in seeking to avoid arrest must at least have been reckless as to causing some harm. Nevertheless, it is obvious that the respective *mens rea* elements for a s.18 offence are significantly unbalanced.

Sentencing

The hierarchy of the non-fatal offences according to seriousness can also be severely criticised. While the maximum punishment for assault and battery is 6 months' imprisonment, an ABH offence under s.47 of the **Offences Against the Person Act 1861** receives a custodial sentence of up to 5 years. Yet the only real difference between the offences is the ABH caused in a s.47 offence — and ABH can mean as little as causing discomfort to the person. In addition, the s.20 offence is defined as much more serious than a s.47 one as regards both its *actus reus* and its *mens rea*, and yet they share the same maximum sentence. It is accepted judicial practice in sentencing that the maximum sentence will rarely be imposed and then only for the most severe type of offence, but the fact remains that the maximum sentences for s.47 and s.20 offences are identical, and it is manifestly unfair that this should be the case when both the *actus reus* and the *mens rea* required for a s.20 conviction are much greater than those for s.47.

A further problem is that the only significant difference between s.20 and s.18 is arguably a slightly more serious *mens rea* under s.18, yet the maximum sentence leaps from 5 years for s.20 to life for s.18. This can perhaps be justified by the fact that a defendant who intends to cause GBH within s.18 has the *mens rea* of murder, and it is merely chance that dictates whether the victim of a stabbing survives or dies.

Constructive intent

The third and possibly most serious criticism that can be directed against the present law is the issue of constructive intent seen in both s.47 and s.20 offences, where the defendant is made liable to a possible 5-year sentence, more because of the outcome — which will, in many cases, have been unforeseen and unintended — than because of the degree of *mens rea*. This runs counter to the basic requirement of criminal liability — that it should depend on, and indeed reflect, the amount of fault, i.e. *mens rea*, possessed by the defendant.

Knowledge check 22

What is meant by constructive intent?

Development of statutory offences through case law

The final argument concerning the present state of the law on non-fatal offences must surely be about the ways in which the statutory offences in the **Offences Against the Person Act 1861** are almost constantly being redefined through reported cases. It is unsatisfactory for so many changes to be made to statutory offences by means of case law, which by its nature can be amended by later cases being appealed to the Court of Appeal or the Supreme Court. This is both an unnecessary and expensive appeals process, arising from wrong decisions on questions of law. The cases of *R* v *Ireland* and *R* v *Burstow* in 1998 have considerably extended the law on assault and s.20 GBH, and *R* v *Dica* (2005) seems to have created a further major extension to the definition of GBH. In the *Dica* case, the defendant was convicted of causing 'biological' GBH when he tricked two women into having unprotected sexual intercourse with him, even though he had been diagnosed with HIV in 1995.

In the Court of Appeal, Dica's conviction was quashed and a retrial was ordered to consider the defence argument of consent. Meanwhile the court ruled that injury by reckless infection in the course of sexual activity does fall within the scope of s.20 of the **Offences Against the Person Act** — unless the alleged victim consents to run the risk.

Even more importantly, the Court of Appeal has apparently widened the scope of the defence of consent in such cases, distinguishing the case of *R* v *Brown* (1994), where this defence was expressly disallowed by the House of Lords. Here, the court ruled that 'there is a vital difference between consenting to the deliberate infliction of harm, and consenting to an activity that you know involves a risk of it'. This ruling means that criminal liability does not arise where the other party knows, or suspects, and is prepared to take the risk.

Proposed law reform

The draft Criminal Law Bill, issued by the Home Office in 1998, based on the Law Commission's recommendations of 5 years earlier and not yet enacted as law, proposes to update the language used for these offences by talking about 'serious injury' rather than 'grievous bodily harm', and avoiding the words 'maliciously' and 'wounding' altogether. Under the bill, s.18 would be replaced by 'intentionally causing serious injury' (for which the maximum penalty would be life imprisonment);

s.20 by 'recklessly causing serious injury' (maximum penalty 7 years); and s.47 by 'intentionally or recklessly causing injury' (maximum penalty 5 years). The bill still uses the term 'assault' for the two separate offences of assault and battery.

Critical evaluation of the law on fatal offences

Murder

When the Law Commission's 2006 report on murder, manslaughter and infanticide declared 'The law governing homicide in England and Wales is a rickety structure set upon shaky foundations', it was stating what many practising and academic lawyers had been arguing for years.

Lack of a codified law

The first severe criticism is that the law on murder is common law, made and developed by judges through reported cases. In all other developed countries, including other common law countries such as the USA, Australia and New Zealand, the law on murder has been codified, usually with different 'degrees' of murder to reflect the graduated levels of fault with which this offence can be committed. Because there is only one 'degree' of murder in England and Wales, there is only one sentence — the mandatory life sentence — and that means judges have limited scope to differentiate between types of murderer. The serial killer receives the same sentence as the gang member who kept a lookout and warned the actual killer of the victim's arrival.

The situation also results in 'mercy-killers' (who in truth are 'murderers') being convicted of the lesser offence of manslaughter by reason of diminished responsibility simply to avoid the mandatory sentence, and in 1989, the report of the Select Committee of the House of Lords on murder and life imprisonment agreed with most of the senior judges who had given evidence to the committee and recommended abolition of this sentence.

When imposing the life sentence, judges do have the power to set a 'tariff' — a minimum term that must be served before the defendant is eligible for parole — but although this allows some measure of differentiation between murderers, it is still the case that a life sentence is precisely that. Even though the great majority of 'lifers' are released early, they are only released on licence, which means they can be returned to prison if they commit any criminal offence later.

Intention

The greatest single criticism of the present law of murder is over the *mens rea*, which is described as malice aforethought, even though no malice (hatred or ill-will) or any premeditation are required. The *mens rea* for murder has been interpreted by judges to mean intention to kill or to commit GBH — see *R* v *Vickers* (1957) — but Professor Glanville Williams has asked: 'Why is it that intention, one of the basic concepts of the criminal law, remains so unclear? Judges decline to define it, and they appear to adjust it from one case to another.' This constant reinterpretation is most obvious in questions of oblique intent, where the definition has changed completely from the cases of *DPP* v *Smith* (1961) to the current situation established in *R* v *Nedrick* (1986), *R* v *Woollin* (1999) and *R* v *Matthews and Alleyne* (2003). The present position is that

Examiner tip

The various difficulties with intention — definition, changes, implied malice — are the most serious criticisms of murder and therefore require to be explained fully.

the jury may find the intent necessary for a murder conviction if it is satisfied that the defendant foresaw death or serious injury as being a virtually certain consequence of his or her voluntary act or acts.

A further critical issue is that of implied malice, where the defendant's intention was to commit GBH. In *R v Vickers*, Lord Goddard CJ defended this level of *mens rea* as always having been sufficient in English law to imply the malice aforethought for murder. However, it does have the unwelcome consequence of making murder in such cases an offence of constructive liability, where the *mens rea* does not correspond with the *actus reus* or with the punishment imposed for the offence. The Criminal Law Revision Committee stated in its 1980 report: 'It is wrong in principle that a person should be liable to be convicted of murder who neither intended nor was reckless as to the most important element in the offence, namely death.'

> **Knowledge check 23**
>
> In which case was it held that intention to cause GBH was sufficient for a murder conviction?

Recommendations for future reform

The Law Commission has accepted these major criticisms and has recommended that there be two degrees of murder. The first degree would require intentional killing, or killing through an intention to do serious injury but with an awareness of a serious risk of causing death. Second-degree murder would involve killing with an intention to do serious injury, or killing where there was an awareness of the risk of causing death coupled with an intention to cause injury, a fear of injury or a risk of injury. If this particular recommendation is passed into law, at a stroke it will resolve the twin issues of the mandatory sentence and the 'intention' problem.

Voluntary manslaughter

The law on voluntary manslaughter has also given rise to considerable criticisms. First, the offence itself is an artificial one, created to enable murderers to escape the gallows on the grounds that their fault in killing was in some way reduced, either because of loss of self-control due to provocation or by diminished responsibility caused by an abnormality of mind. It is noteworthy that the Law Commission has recommended that, in future, defendants who successfully plead provocation or diminished responsibility will be convicted of second-degree murder rather than manslaughter; this acknowledges that the major justification for such defences is to avoid the mandatory life sentence.

Loss of control

While the **Coroners and Justice Act 2009** can certainly be praised for addressing some of the more critical issues in the old law on provocation, it can still be argued that the new defence (like provocation) effectively 'blames' the victim to some extent for his or her own death. It would have been better had the clear recommendation of the Law Commission in its murder report been accepted as to making defendants who successfully plead loss of self-control liable to be convicted of second-degree murder. The inclusion of the 'fear' trigger makes the new rules more 'gender neutral' — under these rules, both Thornton and Ahluwalia would surely have been acquitted of murder. The fact that there is no need for 'a sudden, temporary and immediate loss of control' also removes a considerable stumbling block.

There are, however, new problems created by these new rules. In the first place, it can be argued that the exclusion of the 'considered desire for revenge' is both unnecessary and confusing. Surely a loss of control cannot exist if there is such a considered desire for revenge — they are self-contradictory.

The creation of the new 'fear trigger' goes some way to dealing with the problem that provocation only covered anger responses, and it probably also has the virtue of supplying a defence in self-defence cases where excessive force was used.

A distinction has to be drawn between anticipatory force where the defendant uses force in anticipation of serious violence against him/her or another at some time in the future, and reactive force where the defendant uses force at a time when serious violence is being used or threatened against him/her or another. In cases of anticipatory force, it would be difficult for the defence to prove there was loss of control or to deny there was a 'considered desire for revenge'. Given that the defendant must prove he or she has lost self-control, this defence is far more likely to succeed in cases involving reactive force, but in such cases, self-defence — a full defence — could be available.

Knowledge check 24

What are the two requirements of the 'anger trigger'?

Concerning the 'anger trigger', the two requirements — the circumstances must be extremely grave and the defendant's sense of grievance must arise from a justifiable sense of being seriously wronged — are significantly more challenging than the former tests for provocation. These tests are also more demanding than the 'gross provocation' test recommended by the Law Commission in its murder report.

As for the exclusion of sexual infidelity, Lanser argues: 'this was an unnecessary exclusion which is very poorly drafted. It ought to be possible to exclude undeserving instances of alleged loss of control caused by jealousy, sexual activity etc. simply by reference to the now very much more demanding elements of the anger trigger'. It is to be hoped that the somewhat liberal approach of the decision in *R* v *Clinton* will resolve the problems caused by this problematic exclusion.

Finally, the problem with the objective test remains: although the 'reasonable man' test has been reworded to 'a person of D's sex and age, with a normal degree of tolerance and self-restraint and in the circumstances of D', the central problem is that such a person, even if he or she lost self-control, would be unlikely to kill as a result.

Diminished responsibility

There were a number of serious criticisms directed at the former rules on diminished responsibility. The first was that the burden of proof was on the defendant — this remains the case. Another criticism was the term 'abnormality of mind' and the listing of elements which could cause this — arising from a condition of arrested or retarded development or any inherent cause. These requirements were vague and caused serious problems for psychiatrists and juries alike. The final rule of the former law was the requirement that the abnormality of mind had to 'substantially impair the defendant's mental responsibility for the killing' — this phrase was never clearly explained in any case judgement and must have caused great difficulty to both judges and juries.

Significant reforms were introduced in the **Coroners and Justice Act 2009** which largely address these serious criticisms. The new rules require the defendant to suffer from an abnormality of mental functioning which arose from a recognised medical condition which substantially impaired the defendant's ability '(a) to understand the nature of D's conduct; (b) to form a rational judgement; (c) to exercise self-control.' The final requirement is that this abnormality 'provides an explanation for D's acts and omissions in doing or being a party to the killing'.

While the term 'abnormality of mental functioning' by itself is still unclear, the fact that it has to arise from a recognised medical condition and must have substantially impaired the defendant's ability to do any of the specific elements in s.52 should greatly facilitate the ability of psychiatrists to provide much clearer and more readily understandable evidence to the court. There are, however, the same problems of explaining the rule concerning diminished responsibility and intoxication.

That the statute now provides that there must be a causal link between the abnormality of mental functioning and the defendant's conduct is also welcome as this is the first time that a causal connection has been clearly spelled out and the provision exceeds the recommendations of the Law Commission, which would have stopped at the requirement for the abnormality to provide an explanation, without further elaboration.

All these tests should make it easier for psychiatrists to provide accurate evidence based on psychiatric medical concepts, and thus for juries to be able to evaluate that evidence.

In 'tightening' this particular defence, it may be argued that the 'collusion' between judges, prosecution and defence counsel which permitted 'mercy killers' to escape a murder conviction by permitting this defence to cover such cases will no longer be possible.

Critical evaluation of defences

Consent

The range of this defence has entirely been laid down in common law by judges.

The general rule with this defence is that it is available to the minor crimes of assault and battery, but it is not available in more serious offences from s.47 to s.18 except in particular circumstances. Thus the question has been asked — what are those circumstances which justify the defence of consent? In *Attorney-General's Reference (No. 6 of 1980)*, Lord Lane CJ stated:

> ...nothing which we have said is intended to cast doubt on the accepted legality of properly conducted games and sports, lawful chastisement or correction, reasonable surgical interference, dangerous exhibitions etc. These apparent exceptions can be justified as involving the exercise of a legal right or as needed in the public interest.

It would be better to base this defence on the high value placed on individual autonomy and liberty and then to 'examine reasons why particular consensual activities should be criminalised by way of exception to that general principle of autonomy' rather than 'taking refuge in overblown claims about what is needed in the public interest'. This, of course, was the basis of the controversial decision in *R v Brown* (1994) involving sado-masochistic homosexual activities to which all the men had freely consented and which were carried out in private. Two judges in the House of Lords (Lords Mustill and Slynn) dissented from the majority view, holding that there was no compelling interest in criminalising conduct which was private and consensual and imposed no burden on the health service. However, the majority condemned this behaviour in terms of 'cruelty' and 'violence', finding that these practices fully justified being criminalised. Yet, in *R* v *Wilson*, where far more serious harm was inflicted on the wife when her husband branded her buttocks, it was held that her consent was a full defence. It is difficult to distinguish these contradictory decisions on any grounds other than prejudice against homosexual activities. Indeed, in *Complete Criminal Law*, Janet Loveless wrote: 'the academic literature overwhelmingly casts *Brown* as a moralistic, anti-civil libertarian decision which served to discriminate against a sexual minority'.

Other specific problems emerge from cases such as *R* v *Jones* where, as a result of rough horseplay, two boys suffered serious injuries — a broken arm for one, a ruptured spleen in another — yet, despite these injuries, the defence of consent was allowed. As Janet Loveless said in *Complete Criminal Law*: 'this represents quite a degree of legal tolerance of male violent activities in circumstances where the V is given no real right of refusal'. The court stressed that the criminal law is not concerned with physical contact provided it does not go too far.

Self-defence

At present, self-defence is an all-or-nothing defence. If it is successfully pleaded, the defendant will be acquitted; if not, the defendant will be convicted of the crime charged, and if that is murder, the mandatory life sentence must be imposed. In *R* v *Clegg* (1995), defence counsel argued before the House of Lords that in cases brought against police officers or, as in that particular case, military personnel assisting the civil powers, use of unreasonable force should result in a conviction for involuntary manslaughter instead of murder, but the argument was rejected by the Law Lords, on the grounds that such a change in the law could only be made by Parliament.

Knowledge check 25

In which case was an attempt made to change the law on self-defence in murder cases to enable excessive force to reduce the conviction to manslaughter?

There has also been considerable public concern about the use of lethal force by the police in defence of state security. The mistaken shooting of Jean Charles de Menezes in London in 2005 clearly illustrates the reasons for this concern. Could such a killing be defended using the law on self-defence? And, if so, is such a law compatible with Article 2 — the right to life — in the **European Convention on Human Rights and Fundamental Freedoms** (ECHR)? Article 2 could also make it difficult to use self-defence to justify killing a person in defence of property, or in the more general prevention of crime.

Insanity

The first criticism of the defence of insanity is that the rules were created by judges in 1843, when psychiatric illness was barely understood. Despite huge developments in understanding, diagnosing and treating psychiatric illness, the M'Naghten rules remain unchanged and an insanity plea must satisfy these rules as interpreted by judges. In 1953, the Royal Commission on Capital Punishment described these rules as obsolete and misleading, and the superficiality of 'disease of the mind' as outdated and inaccurate. Given that diminished responsibility has seen major changes in the **Coroners and Justice Act 2009** to reflect medical rather than legal rules, it is absurd that there have been no similar changes to the law on insanity.

The present law can also be criticised for being too wide because it covers epilepsy, sleepwalking and diabetes. At the same time, it is too narrow as it can exclude many defendants who are clinically (but not legally) insane: the defect-of-reason test excludes those who know what they are doing but cannot help themselves.

Psychiatric medicine no longer defines mental disorders as insanity, and a psychiatrist would argue that a person may understand what he or she is doing and still be mentally ill, whereas a judge would hold that a person who is partially rational is not insane and therefore must be held accountable. As is the position with diminished responsibility, it is common for prosecution and defence to lead conflicting expert evidence at trial. If left to the jury by the trial judge, the decision of whether or not the defendant is legally insane is made by medically unqualified jurors, who have to choose between expert psychiatrists.

To detain under the **Criminal Procedure (Insanity and Unfitness to Plead) Act 1991** defendants who are epileptics, diabetics or sleepwalkers could be in breach of Article 5 of the ECHR — the right to liberty. In *Winterwerp* v *Netherlands* (1979), the European Court of Human Rights ruled that whether or not someone is of unsound mind is a matter of objective medical expertise and that detention is unlawful, unless the mental disorder warrants compulsory hospitalisation.

Finally, it can be argued that the M'Naghten rules are contrary to the presumption of innocence enshrined in Article 6 of the ECHR — the right to a fair trial — because the burden of proof is reversed. Since the prosecution is not required to prove *mens rea* in insanity cases, the criticism arises that, if the defendant fails to prove insanity but the prosecution proves the *actus reus*, the defendant can still be convicted, despite the existence of reasonable doubt concerning the *mens rea*.

Intoxication

In *Criminal Law: the Fundamentals*, Rebecca Huxley-Binns writes about the rules concerning intoxication as a defence: 'The law is a mass of inconsistency, lacks any logic and is rooted firmly in policy.'

In *Complete Criminal Law: Texts, Cases and Materials*, Janet Loveless argues that 'the Majewski rule is contrary to three fundamental principles of criminal liability:

> It assumes that recklessness in the ordinary sense of the word is a sufficient substitute for recklessness in the legal sense of the word. The latter requires awareness of the risk of committing the *actus reus* of an offence, whereas the former is a colloquial description of non-criminal conduct. Ashworth notes that, 'in most cases it is far-fetched to argue that a person who is getting drunk is aware of the type of conduct he or she might later indulge in' (*Principles of Criminal Law*).

> It ignores the principle that *actus reus* and *mens rea* should coincide. The recklessness in becoming drunk will usually occur before the crime is committed.

> It is contrary to the general principle that *mens rea* must be proved by the prosecution. It also runs counter to s.8 Criminal Justice Act 1967, which requires juries to consider the defendant's subjective state of mind. Clearly, if the defendant is so intoxicated as to not know what he is doing or fails to foresee something that they ordinarily would not miss, the defendant will have no 'state of mind' that could be described as one of *mens rea*.

Knowledge check 26

Which case suggests that the detention of diabetics, epileptics or sleepwalkers could breach Article 5 of the ECHR?

A further criticism of the *Majewski* rule lies in the distinction it makes between crimes of basic and specific intent. It assumes that this distinction is always easy to draw, when this is simply not the case. Another problem arises with that part of the rule that allows the defendant to be convicted of a basic-intent offence if intoxication is accepted as a partial defence to a specific-intent crime. This functions in murder, where the defendant can be convicted of involuntary manslaughter, but in theft — a crime of specific intent — there is no lesser basic-intent offence.

Summary

Evaluation of the law on non-fatal offences

- not fully codified
- badly defined
- archaic language, e.g. grievous
- constructive liability in ss.47 and 20
- illogical sentencing
- excessive case-made law
- reforms — see Law Commission recommendations

Evaluation of the law on fatal offences

Murder

- still not codified
- intention remains a serious problem — oblique intent definition and implied malice
- mandatory life sentence, but note tariff system
- reforms — see Law Commission report; main reform — two degrees of murder

Voluntary manslaughter

Loss of self-control:

- improvements — no need for immediate loss of control
- addition of 'fear' trigger makes it more 'gender neutral'
- 'anger' trigger requirements much more difficult to achieve
- exclusion of the 'considered desire for revenge' is both unnecessary and confusing
- problem with interpretation of 'sexual infidelity'
- objective test remains unrealistic
- development and interpretation through case law required

Diminished responsibility:

- Law now much more focused on medical rather than legal terms — recognised medical condition now required, and specific tests on substantial impairment.

- Burden of proof still rests on defendant — must be a causal link between the abnormality of mental functioning and defendant's conduct.
- New tighter rules will probably exclude mercy-killers being able to use this defence.

Evaluation of defences

Consent:

- all judge-made law
- difficult to understand different decisions in *R v Brown* and *R v Wilson*
- problem with rough horseplay exception, especially if serious injury caused, e.g. *R v Jones*

Self-defence:

- 'all or nothing defence'
- 'reasonable force' gives juries too much scope in decision making
- issue of 'genuine' belief, rather than 'reasonable' belief
- conflict with ECHR, especially if force used to prevent property crime

Insanity:

- M'Naghten rules created by judges in 1843 — despite major advances in diagnosis and treatment of psychiatric conditions, law still not changed.
- Conditions such as epilepsy, sleepwalking and even diabetes can be included within these rules.
- Conflict with ECHR over burden of proof placed on defendant, and with issue of right to liberty.

Intoxication:

- 'The law is a mass of inconsistency, lacks any logic and is rooted firmly in policy.'
- Distinction between specific and basic intent offences is difficult to define.
- Majewski rules run counter to basic principles of criminal liability.

Section B: Contract law

Formation of contract

In order to be valid, a contract must meet certain conditions, such as an offer and an acceptance, and these have to be present when it is formed. Bilateral contracts involve one party making an offer and another party indicating acceptance either orally or in writing. Unilateral contracts are where only one party is making a promise; an example is the case of *Carlill* v *Carbolic Smoke Ball Company* (1893), where one party made an offer but acceptance was through the performance of an act, rather than through a formal indication of acceptance.

Offer

An offer is defined as an expression of willingness to contract on certain terms, made with the intention that it will become binding on acceptance. An offer may be express or it may be implied from conduct, as when taking goods to the checkout in a supermarket.

An offer can be specific (made to one person or group of people, in which case it can only be accepted by that person or group) or it can be general and not limited as to whom it is directed at. An offer of a reward is a good example of a general offer, as in *Carlill* v *Carbolic Smoke Ball Company*. A more recent example is *Bowerman* v *ABTA* (1996), where the offer was that any holiday booked with a particular tour operator would be guaranteed by the Association of British Travel Agents if the tour operator ceased trading.

Examples of offers

- Reward posters and advertisements are offers, so long as it is clear that all that needs to be done is to fulfil certain conditions, as happened in *Carlill* v *Carbolic Smoke Ball Company*.
- Promotional campaigns, such as a supermarket's campaign to encourage customers to buy one product and get another free, are offers.

Invitations to treat

An 'invitation to treat' is a preliminary stage at which someone is invited to make an offer. Whether something is an offer or an invitation will depend on all the circumstances.

The following are invitations to treat:
- displays of goods in shop windows, as in *Fisher* v *Bell* (1961)
- displays of goods in self-service stores, as in *Pharmaceutical Society* v *Boots* (1953)
- small advertisements, for example in magazines or newspapers, as in *Partridge* v *Crittenden* (1968)
- price lists, catalogues, circulars and timetables
- responses to requests for information, as in *Harvey* v *Facey* (1983), *Gibson* v *Manchester City Council* (1979)
- auction sales, as in *British Car Auctions* v *Wright* (1972)
- invitations to tender

Knowledge check 27

What is an offer?

Examiner tip
It is important to be able to recognise when a question expects you to discuss offer and acceptance. The clue will usually be that there are various stages of negotiation before a final agreement. Some questions on the other hand may refer to someone seeing an advertisement and then signing a contract. In situations like this there is no need to discuss offer and acceptance.

Possible offers

The law as to what constitutes an offer with regard to public transport and timetables remains unclear, but in *Wilkie* v *London Passenger Transport Board* (1947), it was suggested that the offer is made by running the service and the offer is accepted when the passenger gets on board.

Further rules about offers

- The offer must be certain, i.e. its terms must be clear and definite without any ambiguity.
- The offer can be made by any method. It can be made in writing, orally or by conduct (for example by picking up an item and taking it to the cash desk).
- The offer can be made to anyone — to an individual, a group, a company or organisation, and even, as in *Carlill* v *Carbolic Smoke Ball Company*, to the whole world. As Lindley LJ commented in *Carlill*: 'The offer is to anybody who performs the conditions named in the advertisement.'
- The offer must be communicated because a person cannot accept what he or she does not know about.
- The offer must still be in existence when it is accepted. Any revocation must be received before the acceptance is made.

Termination of offers

An offer can be brought to an end at any point before acceptance in a number of different ways:

- **By acceptance or refusal:** acceptance may be in writing, orally or by conduct. If an offer is refused, it is ended, which means that it cannot be accepted later if there is a change of mind.
- **By failure of a precondition:** some offers are made subject to certain conditions, as when a person offers to sell his or her car if he or she is given a company car.
- **By a counter-offer:** as in *Hyde* v *Wrench* (1840).
- **By revocation:** withdrawal of the offer must be communicated, but that can be by a third party, as in *Dickinson* v *Dodds* (1876). The revocation must be received before the acceptance is made, as illustrated in *Byrne* v *Van Tienhoven* (1880). It seems that a revocation will be valid if it is delivered to the last known address. This would also appear to be the position if the revocation is sent by fax or telex during office hours but is not read until some time later. Where the offer is to enter into a unilateral contract, the revocation must take place before performance has begun; an exception to this rule is the promise to pay commission to estate agents for the sale of a property. To revoke an offer made to the public at large, it is probably sufficient to take reasonable steps to draw it to the attention of those at whom the original offer was directed.
- **By lapse of time:** where no time limit is specified, the offer will remain open for a reasonable time; see *Ramsgate Victoria Hotel* v *Montefiore* (1866). What is considered reasonable will depend on the circumstances: for example, an offer to sell perishable goods may lapse in a few days. If a time limit is specified, it must be complied with.

- **By the death of the person making the offer:** it has been suggested that the death of either party terminates the offer, as it makes it impossible for the parties to reach agreement.

Acceptance

Acceptance is unqualified and unconditional agreement by words or conduct to all the terms of the offer. If conditions or qualifications are added, a counter-offer is created; see *Tinn* v *Hoffman* (1873).

Knowledge check 28

What is the main case that illustrates counter-offer?

Rules on acceptance

Acceptance must be communicated. Mere silence cannot amount to acceptance, unless it is absolutely clear that acceptance was intended; see *Felthouse* v *Bindley* (1862). Acceptance can be inferred from conduct. The principle seems to be that when you start to implement what is in the offer, you have accepted, but the courts will interpret conduct as indicating acceptance only if it seems reasonable to infer that acceptance was intended, as happened in *Brogden* v *Metropolitan Rail Co.* (1877).

Methods of acceptance

If a method of acceptance is specified, it must be complied with, but in some circumstances another, equally good, method may suffice. In *Tinn* v *Hoffman*, acceptance was requested by return of post, but the court held that 'any other means not later than a letter written by return of post' could be used. If no method is specified, any method will do, as long as it is effective. However, where an offer is made by an instantaneous method, such as e-mail, fax or telephone, an acceptance by post would not usually be considered reasonable.

The 'postal rule' applies when ordinary letter post is used. This means that acceptance is valid when posted, even if the letter is lost in the post, but a revocation of an offer is valid only when it is received; see *Adams* v *Lindsell* (1818), *Household Fire Insurance* v *Grant* (1879) and *Henthorn* v *Fraser* (1892). The postal rule does not apply where the person making the offer has specified that acceptance must be directly communicated, as in *Holwell Securities Ltd* v *Hughes* (1974).

Instantaneous methods

When instantaneous methods such as telephone, fax or telex are used, acceptance is immediate so long as the message is actually received; see *Entores* v *Miles Far East Corporation* (1955) and *Brinkibon* v *Stahag Stahl* (1983).

Knowledge check 29

What is the rule with acceptance by instantaneous methods?

Standard form contracts

If an offer is made by a business using its own standard form and the business receiving the offer alters the terms by sending back its own form, that second form amounts to a counter-offer. What may then follow is a series of communications, with each party referring to its own terms. The general rule in such cases is that the 'last shot' wins the battle; see *British Road Services* v *Arthur V. Crutchley and Co.* (1968) and contrast with *Butler Machine Tool Co.* v *Ex-Cell-O Corporation* (1979).

Consideration

Consideration is something of value being offered by each party. Sometimes it can be of little value, and it does not have to correspond to the actual worth of what the other party offers. Consideration was defined in *Currie* v *Misa* (1875) as 'some right, interest, profit or benefit accruing to one party, or some forbearance, detriment, loss or responsibility given, suffered or undertaken by the other'.

Types of consideration

Consideration can, and often does, involve a promise by the parties to do something in the future, and this exchange of promises is called **executory consideration**. In unilateral contracts, however, the party making the offer, for example of a reward, is under no obligation until the other party performs (executes) his or her part of the agreement. This is called **executed consideration**.

Knowledge check 30

What is executory consideration?

Rules of consideration

- Something of value must be given by all the parties. This distinguishes a contract from a purely gratuitous agreement, i.e. a promise to make a gift. The law says that consideration must be sufficient. This means that it must be real and tangible and have some actual value.
- It does not have to be adequate, i.e. the market price. The courts will not investigate contracts to see if the parties have got equal value; see *Thomas* v *Thomas* (1842) and *Chappell and Co. Ltd* v *Nestlé Co. Ltd* (1959).
- It must not be past. Any consideration must come after the agreement, rather than being something that has already been done. For example, if A paints B's house and after the work is finished, B promises to pay £100 for it, this promise is unenforceable because A's consideration is past. An example is *Re McArdle* (1951). The law recognises, however, that there are situations in which something, for example a restaurant meal or a taxi ride, is provided on the unspoken expectation that ultimately it will be paid for. This principle is known as the rule in *Lampleigh* v *Braithwaite* (1615) and was applied in *Re Casey's Patent* (1892).
- It must not be an existing duty. Doing something that you are already bound to do cannot amount to good consideration; see *Stilk* v *Myrick* (1809) and contrast *Hartley* v *Ponsonby* (1857). The modern example of *Williams* v *Roffey* (1990) seems to indicate that, as regards business contracts, the courts will try to find consideration in circumstances where, on the face of it, the consideration appears to be part of an existing duty. In other duty situations, such as *Glasbrook Brothers* v *Glamorgan County Council* (1925) and *Harris* v *Sheffield United Football Club* (1988), the courts have also been prepared to find evidence of consideration. A promise to do something as part of a contract, which the party is already obliged to do under a contract with a third party, can be good consideration: see *Scotson* v *Pegg* (1861).
- Part-payment of a debt cannot be consideration for the whole debt — see Pinnel's Case (1602) — unless something else is offered as consideration. There are, however, a number of exceptions to this rule.
- The **Contracts (Rights of Third Parties) Act 1999** has significantly altered the position of third parties who are beneficiaries of contracts. In the past, such contracts would not have been enforceable by the third parties as they had not supplied

consideration; see *Tweddle* v *Atkinson*. Now s.1(1) of the 1999 Act allows a third party to enforce a contract if it contains an express term to that effect or if the contract purports to confer a benefit on a third party. The Act allows enforcement only where the benefit is intended for a specific person or for a member of a specific group and where it is clear that the parties intended the benefit to be enforceable by the third party.

Knowledge check 31

What does s.1(1) of the Contracts (Rights of Third Parties) Act 1999 allow?

Privity of contract

Privity of contract means that only a party to a contract can sue on it. This principle was set out by Viscount Haldane LC in *Dunlop Pneumatic Tyre Co.* v *Selfridge and Co.* (1915). There are a number of exceptions to the rule:

- Parliament is able to legislate to create third-party rights.
- Restrictive covenants bind subsequent purchasers, even though they were not parties to the original agreement; see *Tulk* v *Moxhay* (1848).
- Creation of a trust avoids the strict application of privity of contract, although the courts have been reluctant to accept that a trust exists when it is not explicitly stated.
- Where a collateral contract may be said to exist, as in *Shanklin Pier* v *Detel Products Ltd* (1951), privity of contract may be avoided.
- The court may identify a number of related contracts indicating a clear intention that benefits under the contract in question were to be shared between members of a family or of some other group; see *Jackson* v *Horizon Holidays* (1975), although this was not approved by the House of Lords in *Woodar Investment Development Ltd* v *Wimpey Construction Ltd* (1980).
- The **Contracts (Rights of Third Parties) Act 1999** allows a third party to enforce a contract as discussed above.

Examiner tip

Watch out for questions involving third parties. Where you are asked to consider the rights of a third party (e.g. someone for whom something has been bought) do not forget to discuss the impact of the 1999 Act.

Intention to create legal relations

Social and domestic agreements

Case law suggests that agreements within families will not generally be treated as legally binding; see *Jones* v *Padavatton* (1969). Contrast *Balfour* v *Balfour* (1919) and *Merritt* v *Merritt* (1970). In cases that do not simply involve members of the same family, any presumption that the arrangement is a purely social one will be rebutted if money has changed hands; see *Simpkins* v *Pays* (1955), *Peck* v *Lateu* (1973) and *Parker* v *Clarke* (1960).

Examiner tip

Note that these are presumptions. Care needs to be taken in exam questions involving friends or neighbours to discuss whether the facts show there is intention to create legal relations.

Commercial and business agreements

There is a strong presumption that in commercial agreements, the parties intend to be legally bound, as was confirmed in *Esso Petroleum* v *Customs and Excise Commissioners* (1976). There are, however, a number of circumstances in which a different intent can be shown: honour clauses are one such exception (see *Roes and Frane* v *Crompton Bros*, 1925), and football pools (as in *Jones* v *Vernon Pools*, 1938) are another. Situations where free gifts or prizes are promised are deemed to be legally binding because the purpose is to promote the commercial interests of the body offering the gift or prize; see *McGowan* v *Radio Buxton* (2001). In *Edwards* v *Skyways* (1964), an ex-gratia payment, i.e. a gift, by an airline was held to be related to business matters and was presumed to be binding.

Summary

To be valid a contract must have:

- **Offer** — the expression of a willingness to enter into a legally binding agreement:
  - can be made to individual or group
  - must be certain
  - can be made by any method to anyone
  - must be in existence when accepted
  - must be distinguished from invitation to treat
  - can be terminated by refusal/counter-offer/revocation/lapse of time
- **Acceptance** — unqualified and unconditional acceptance of all terms in the offer:
  - must be communicated, though it can be inferred from conduct
  - must be by method specified or one as good as
  - if no method specified, can be by any method as long as it is effective
  - postal rule applies to acceptance using post
  - acceptance is immediate if instantaneous methods used
- **Consideration:**
  - must have some value
  - must not be past
  - must not be existing duty
- **Intention to create legal relations** — presumed in commercial and business agreements but not in social or domestic arrangements

Contract terms

Statements that are incorporated into the contract and by which the parties intend to be bound are known as **terms**. A statement intended to induce or persuade a party to enter into a contract is not a term, but a **representation**, and so long as it is not incorporated into the contract, it remains a representation. It should be noted, however, that, because of the **Misrepresentation Act 1967**, this distinction is of less practical significance than it was.

In order to become a term, a statement must be incorporated and form part of the contract. Whether or not it is incorporated depends on a number of factors:

- If a party attaches importance to a statement and has relied on it when deciding to enter into the contract, it will probably be treated as forming part of the contract, as in *Birch* v *Paramount Estates Ltd* (1956).
- The courts are more likely to treat a statement by an expert as incorporated into the contract than a statement by someone without specialist knowledge. Contrast *Oscar Chess Ltd* v *Williams* (1957) and *Dick Bentley Productions Ltd* v *Harold Smith Motors Ltd* (1965).
- The nearer in time the statement is to the formation of the contract, the more likely the court is to treat it as having been incorporated; see *Routledge* v *McKay* (1954).
- A statement is more likely to be deemed a term if it is in writing.
- The more the statement has been drawn to the other party's attention, the more likely it is to be regarded as a term.
- Under the 'parol evidence' rule, oral or other evidence that a party tries to introduce into a written agreement is not admissible to add to, vary or contradict the terms in the written contract; see *Henderson* v *Arthur* (1907). However, there are occasions when strict enforcement of this rule is not appropriate, for example where it is unfair because one party is trying to take advantage of the other's mistake, as in *Webster* v *Cecil* (1861). A collateral contract is another way in which

an oral statement can be deemed to be a term, and therefore binding, even though it conflicts with a written statement.

Conditions and warranties

Conditions are terms that are fundamental to the contract, that go to its root. A breach of a condition will give the injured party the choice of either repudiating (ending) the contract or continuing with it and claiming damages.

Warranties are less important terms and, if broken, entitle an injured party only to damages.

Is a term a condition or warranty?

- The distinction between conditions and warranties can be illustrated by two cases involving opera singers. In *Bettini* v *Gye* (1876), the breach was minor and was therefore treated as a warranty, while in *Poussard* v *Spiers and Pond* (1876), the breach was an important one and was treated as a condition.
- Written contracts may specify that particular terms are conditions, and this is likely to reflect the intention of the parties to treat certain terms as more important than others, as in *Lombard North Central* v *Butterworth* (1987). The courts, however, are not bound to treat the terms in the way a contract describes them. An example is *L Schuler AG* v *Wickman Machine Tool Sales* (1973).
- The implied terms in sections 12–15 of the **Sale of Goods Act 1979** (as amended) are described in the statute as conditions or warranties. These statutory provisions are not negotiable and it is not open to the parties or the courts to alter their status.
- If the parties themselves do not label terms as conditions or warranties, the courts decide the matter on a case-by-case basis.

Innominate terms

Following the decision of the Court of Appeal in *Hong Kong Fir Shipping Co.* v *Kawasaki Kisen Kaisha Ltd* (1962), contracts may also include innominate terms. These are terms that will be treated as conditions in the event of a serious breach and as warranties when the breach is minor.

Express terms

Wherever possible, when the courts have to determine the meaning of a contractual term, words are given their natural and ordinary meaning, but sometimes the courts will look beyond this when a strict interpretation goes against what seems to be a sensible interpretation. In a number of recent decisions, the Law Lords, and Lord Hoffmann in particular, have developed an approach characterised by flexibility and a desire to find the meaning that would make sense to a reasonable person; see, for example, *Sirius International Insurance Co.* v *FAI General Insurance Ltd* (2004).

Implied terms

Terms that are implied are those that, it is assumed, both parties would have intended to include if they had thought about it. They may have thought that a particular term was so obvious that it was not necessary to refer to it or they may have left it out by mistake.

Knowledge check 32
Explain the difference between a term and a representation.

Knowledge check 33
Why is it important to decide whether a term is a condition or a warranty?

Examiner tip
In every contract there will be express terms and exam questions will want you to consider these as well as looking to see if there are any implied terms. Remember that a breach of an express term will be treated as a breach of contract and entitle the injured party to damages or, if treated as a breach of condition, to possible repudiation.

The law has developed two tests to determine whether a term should be written into a contract. The first is known as the 'officious bystander' test — whether the term is one that a third party, standing by, would have thought was obviously intended by the contracting parties. The test originates from remarks by MacKinnon LJ in *Shirlaw* v *Southern Foundries* (1939). He said that a term may be implied 'if it is so obvious that it goes without saying'. One situation in which the 'officious bystander' test cannot be used is where one of the parties would not have understood the term if it had been there, as in *Spring* v *National Amalgamated Stevedores and Dockers Society* (1956). Another situation where the test will not apply is where it is clear that one of the parties would not have agreed to the term if it had been discussed; see *Luxor (Eastbourne) Ltd* v *Cooper* (1941).

The other test is the business efficiency test, where the question is whether a term must be implied in order for the contract to work as an effective business arrangement. The leading case is *The Moorcock* (1889).

Terms implied by custom or trade usage

Terms can be implied if there is evidence that, under local custom, they would normally be there, or if they would routinely be part of a contract in a particular type of trade or business, as in *British Crane Hire Corporation Ltd* v *Ipswich Plant Hire Ltd* (1975).

Implied terms created by statute

Implied terms have also been created by statute. Section 2(1) of the **Sale of Goods Act 1979**, for example, which applies to a sale of goods, defines a contract of sale of goods as 'a contract by which the seller transfers or agrees to transfer the property in goods to the buyer for a money consideration, called the price'. The term 'goods' has been interpreted to include packaging and any instructions appearing on the packaging. Certain provisions of the Act apply only when goods are sold 'in the course of a business'. In *Stevenson* v *Rogers* (1999), a fisherman, whose normal business was selling fish, sold his boat. The Court of Appeal held that this was still a sale in the course of a business.

Section 12(1) of the 1979 Act says that, in a contract of sale, there is an implied term that the seller has the right to sell the goods and is able to pass good title; see *Rowland* v *Divall* (1923). Section 13(1) provides that, where there is a sale of goods by description, there is an implied term that the goods will correspond with the description, as illustrated in *Beale* v *Taylor* (1967) and *Varley* v *Whipp* (1900). However, there must be reliance on the description; see *Harlington and Leinster Enterprises* v *Christopher Hull Fine Art* (1991). Enforcement of s.13 is strict, as illustrated by *Re Moore and Landauer* (1921), but *Reardon Smith Line* v *Hansen-Tangen* (1976) suggests that a trivial breach of description would not be sufficient to allow a party to repudiate the contract. Note that this implied term is not limited to sales in the course of business and therefore also applies to private sales.

Knowledge check 34

Under the 1994 Act what is meant by 'satisfactory quality'?

Section 14(2) of the 1979 Act, as amended by s.1 of the **Sale and Supply of Goods Act 1994**, says that where a seller sells goods in the course of a business, there is an implied term that the goods are of satisfactory quality. Note that this does not apply to private sales. Under s.14(2)(a), 'goods are of satisfactory quality if they meet the standard that a reasonable person would regard as satisfactory, taking account of any description of the goods, the price (if relevant) and all the other relevant circumstances'. Potentially relevant factors outlined under s.14(2)(b) are: fitness for the purpose for which goods of this kind are commonly supplied, finish and appearance, freedom from minor defects, safety and durability. Cases illustrating 'satisfactory quality' are *Priest* v *Last* (1903) and *Bartlett* v *Sidney Marcus* (1965).

In *Brown* v *Craiks* (1970), Lord Reid commented that if you pay a higher price, then you can expect higher quality. This was confirmed in *Clegg* v *Andersson* (2003). The goods need to be satisfactory in their entirety; see *Wilson* v *Rickett, Cockerell and Co.* (1954). A buyer cannot later claim that goods are unsatisfactory if the defect is specifically brought to his or her attention before the contract is made or if he or she examines the goods (or a sample of them if it is a contract for sale by sample) before contracting, and the defect is one that he or she should have discovered on examining them (s.14(2)(c)). This is illustrated by *Bramhill* v *Edwards* (2004).

Section 14(3) states that there is an implied term that goods are fit for any purpose that the buyer specifically makes known to the seller, unless the buyer does not rely on the seller's judgement or it would be unreasonable for him or her to do so; see *Griffiths* v *Peter Conway* (1939). This section applies only to sales in the course of a business and not to private sales.

Section 15 says that there are implied terms that where goods are sold by sample, the bulk must correspond to sample, and that the goods will be free from any defect making their quality unsatisfactory that would not be apparent on reasonable examination of the sample.

The **Supply of Goods and Services Act 1982** extends the protection of implied terms under the **Sale of Goods Act 1979** to goods supplied as part of a service and also to goods that are hired. In addition, it sets out implied terms in relation to contracts for services. Where goods are supplied as part of a service, the implied terms specified in the Sale of Goods Act apply to the goods. For example, the paint and wallpaper used by a decorator or the fittings installed by a plumber are now covered by the Sale of Goods Act implied terms, which are restated in the 1982 Act (with title covered by s.2, description by s.3, satisfactory quality and fitness for purpose by s.4 and sample by s.5). In sections 7–10, the same implied terms are extended to any contract for hire of goods, for example the hire of a car or a television. There are some situations where it is not clear whether a contract is for the sale of goods or for services. Contrast *Lockett* v *A and M Charles Ltd* (1938) and *Robinson* v *Graves* (1935).

Under sections 13–15 of the **Supply of Goods and Services Act 1982**, certain specific terms are automatically implied in service contracts. These are referred to in the Act simply as terms rather than as conditions. They are therefore treated by the courts as innominate terms, and the consequences of a breach depend on how serious that breach is. Section 13 provides: 'In a contract for the supply of a service where the supplier is acting in the course of a business, there is an implied term the supplier will carry out the service with reasonable care and skill.' The reasonableness standard is similar to that used in cases of negligence and essentially requires the consumer to show not that a service was defective, but rather that the provider was at fault in the way it was provided; see *Wilson* v *Best Travel* (1993).

Examiner tip

Make sure when answering a question that you are clear whether it is a contract for supply of goods or a contract for services. A different set of implied terms applies to services, although the Sale of Goods Act terms apply to any goods supplied as part of the service.

Section 14 creates the duty to carry out the service within a reasonable time. What is a reasonable time is a question of fact; see *Charnock* v *Liverpool Corporation* (1968). Section 15 implies a term that, where the price has not been provided for by the contract or by a course of dealing, the customer will pay the supplier a reasonable charge. What is a reasonable charge is a question of fact.

Exclusion of implied terms

Under the **Unfair Contract Terms Act 1977**, s.12 of the **Sale of Goods Act 1979** (as amended) cannot be excluded from any contract, while sections 13–15 cannot be excluded from consumer contracts, and can only be excluded from other contracts if this is reasonable.

Remedies for breach of implied terms

Right to repudiate

A breach of a **Sale of Goods Act** implied term is a breach of condition, and allows the purchaser to reject the goods and demand the return of the purchase price. This right to reject is lost once the goods have been accepted, and the claim then is limited to damages; see s.11(4) of the 1979 Act. Section 61 provides that the remedy in such cases is damages.

Knowledge check 35

What does repudiating a contract allow?

Under s.35, acceptance occurs when the buyer intimates acceptance to the seller, when the buyer does something inconsistent with the seller's ownership after he or she has had a chance to examine the goods (as in the 1893 case of *Perkins* v *Bell*), or when the buyer retains the goods after the lapse of a reasonable time without indicating to the seller that he or she is rejecting them. Sections 2(5) and 2(6) of the **Sale and Supply of Goods Act 1994** state that the buyer must have reasonable opportunity to examine goods and that even having goods repaired by or under arrangement with the seller may not amount to acceptance. Contrasting cases on the treatment of acceptance are *Bernstein* v *Pamson Motors* (1987) and *Rogers* v *Parish (Scarborough) Ltd* (1987).

Examiner tip

Notice that the Sale of Goods Act implied terms are described as conditions and breaches automatically allow the purchaser to repudiate the contract, but breaches of the terms relating to the supply of services are treated as innominate terms and repudiation will only be possible if the breach is regarded as serious.

Under s.3 of the **Sale and Supply of Goods Act 1994**, there is a right of partial rejection where a defect affects only some of the goods and the buyer accepts the remainder.

Section 15(a) of the Act also added the provision that in consumer sales, the right to reject is lost when the breach is so slight that rejection would be unreasonable.

Because the terms in the **Supply of Goods and Services Act** are innominate terms, they do not automatically give rise to a right to repudiate. The courts will consider how serious the breach is before deciding whether repudiation would be appropriate.

Right to damages

Damages may be more appropriate than rejection when supplies of a product are limited and buying an alternative is difficult, or where consumers have suffered personal injury because of a faulty product and wish to sue for consequential loss. The consumer will often be awarded sums far exceeding the value of the product itself, as in *Grant* v *Australian Knitting Mills* (1936) and *Godley* v *Perry* (1960). Another circumstance where damages may be appropriate is where the consumer has lost the right to reject by virtue of accepting the product.

Additional remedies

The **Sale and Supply of Goods to Consumers Regulations 2002** set out four additional remedies: repair; replacement; price reduction; and a full refund (known as rescission). These remedies are now contained in sections 48A–48F of the 1979 Act. The breach must occur within 6 months of purchase, but there is not a time limit on when repair/replacement can be requested. The consumer is not entitled to repair or replacement where this would be impossible or disproportionate. Any remedy must be completed without significant inconvenience to the consumer, and if neither repair nor replacement is realistically possible, consumers can request instead a partial or full refund, depending on what is reasonable in the circumstances. Note that even if the buyer is deemed to have accepted the goods under s.35 and thus to have lost the right to reject, this will not prejudice the buyer's remedies under s.48.

Exemption clauses

Exemption clauses are terms in a contract that seek to exclude all liability in certain events or to limit the liability of one of the parties to a specific amount of money smaller than any reasonable pre-estimate of loss. They can be part of a prewritten document or a separate notice, or even agreed by the parties orally. Suppliers of goods and services often seek to exclude or limit their possible legal liability by the insertion of these clauses in their standard form contracts.

Common law controls

Where an exemption clause is contained in a document that has been signed, it automatically forms part of the contract. The signer is presumed to have read and understood the significance of all the terms contained in the document. This is known as the rule in *L'Estrange* v *Graucob* (1934). Note that this rule will not be held to apply if the other party has misrepresented the terms of the agreement, as happened in *Curtis* v *Chemical Cleaning and Dyeing Co.* (1951). For a signature to be effective in incorporating terms, the document signed must be regarded as contractual. A mere receipt or piece of paper for some other purpose is not enough. The exemption clause may also be contained in an unsigned document such as a ticket or notice, but in those cases the burden of showing that the terms have been incorporated is on the party seeking to rely on them.

For exemption clauses to be effective, the document containing them must be capable of being regarded by a reasonable person as contractual in nature and, as such, likely to contain exemption clauses; see *Chapelton* v *Barry UDC* (1940) and contrast *Parker* v *SE Railway* (1877). The person seeking to rely on the exemption clause must show that reasonable steps have been taken to give notice of the clause to the other contracting party. Denning LJ commented in *Spurling* v *Bradshaw* (1956):

> ...the more unreasonable a clause is, the greater the notice which must be given of it. Some clauses would need to be printed in red ink with a red hand pointing to it before the notice could be held to be sufficient.

Examiner tip
You will be expected to discuss exemption clauses if a question refers to wording which limits a person's rights or places restrictions on the remedy that they might be able to use.

Exemption clauses will also be ineffective unless notice of them is given before the contract is made or at the time the contact is made; see *Chapelton* v *Barry UDC*, *Olley* v *Marlborough Court Ltd* (1949) and *Thornton* v *Shoe Lane Car Parking Ltd* (1971). In *Hollier* v *Rambler Motors Ltd* (1972), a garage tried to rely on an exclusion clause in a notice displayed inside the garage, but the court decided that the customer did not go to the garage frequently enough to have established a course of dealings within which he would have had the opportunity to read the terms.

Where an exemption clause is duly incorporated into a contract, the courts will proceed to examine the words used to see if the clause covers the breach and loss that have occurred. An exemption clause will be effective only if it expressly covers the kind of liability that has, in fact, arisen. If there is any ambiguity or doubt as to the meaning of an exemption clause, the court will interpret it *contra proferentem*, i.e. against the interests of the person seeking to rely on it; see *Houghton* v *Trafalgar Insurance Co.* (1954).

Unfair Contract Terms Act 1977

The **Unfair Contract Terms Act 1977** is the most important piece of legislation affecting exemption clauses: it applies to contract terms and to notices that are non-contractual and purport to exclude or restrict liability in tort. Most of the Act's provisions apply only to things done in the course of business or arising from the occupation of premises used for business purposes (the term 'business' including the professions, government and local and public authorities). Many of the provisions apply only where one of the parties is contracting as a consumer. Under s.12(1), a person 'deals as a consumer' if:

(a) he or she does not make the contract in the course of a business or represent that he or she is doing so

(b) the other party does make the contract in the course of a business

(c) the goods are of a type ordinarily supplied for private use or consumption

In *Peter Symmons and Co.* v *Cook* (1981), the sale of a Rolls-Royce to a firm of surveyors was held to be a consumer sale.

Exemption clauses void under the 1977 Act

- In a consumer sale, s.6 of the 1977 Act, as amended, makes void any clause that tries to exclude or limit the implied terms in the **Sale of Goods Act 1979**.
- In any contract, s.6 of the 1977 Act, as amended, makes void any clause that tries to exclude or limit the implied term relating to title under s.12 of the **Sale of Goods Act 1979**.
- In a consumer sale, s.6 of the 1977 Act makes void exemption clauses relating to implied terms as to description (under s.13 of the **Sale of Goods Act 1979**), satisfactory quality (s.14(2) of the 1979 Act), fitness for purpose (s.14(3)) and sample corresponding with bulk (s.15). Section 6(4) extends the application of s.6 to hire purchase agreements.
- Section 2 of the 1977 Act makes void clauses in any contract, or any non-contractual notice, seeking to exempt liability for death or injury caused by negligence. This particularly applies to situations involving the provision of a service where there is an attempt to exclude s.13 of the **Supply of Goods and Services Act 1982**, which requires work to be done with reasonable care and skill.

- Section 5 of the 1977 Act makes void a manufacturer's guarantee seeking to exempt liability for loss or damage caused by defects in the goods while they are in consumer use.

Exemption clauses that seek to exclude or limit liability for negligent loss or damage in consumer contracts or between businesses will be valid only if reasonable (s.2 of the 1977 Act). Exemption clauses in contracts between businesses that seek to exclude or limit implied terms will also be valid only if reasonable (s.6(3)). This also applies to certain other clauses in consumer contracts or contracts between businesses where written standard terms are used (s.3) and to clauses that seek to exclude or restrict liability for misrepresentation (s.8).

What is reasonable?

The test of reasonableness is found in s.11 and Schedule 2 of the 1977 Act. The burden of proof is on the party inserting the clause to show that it is reasonable in all the circumstances, as illustrated in *Warren* v *Truprint Ltd* (1986). Under s.11(1), the court should ask whether the term is fair and reasonable, 'having regard to the circumstances which were, or ought reasonably to have been, known to or in the contemplation of the parties when the contract was made'. Schedule 2 of the Act refers to some potentially relevant issues, including the relative strength of the parties' bargaining positions and whether the customer received an inducement to agree to the term (for example a cheaper price). *Smith* v *Eric Bush* (1990), *Green* v *Cade* (1978) and *George Mitchell* v *Finney Lock Seeds* (1983) are cases where clauses were held to be unreasonable. In *Watford Electronics* v *Sanderson* (2001), the clause was found to be reasonable.

Generally, exemption clauses in consumer contracts are less likely than those in business contracts to satisfy the test of reasonableness, but if they are well drafted and placed in the right context, they may be held to be reasonable, as in *Woodman* v *Photo Trade Processing* (1981).

> **Knowledge check 36**
>
> What is the main legislative measure that regulates exemption clauses?

The Unfair Terms in Consumer Contracts Regulations 1999

These 1999 rules apply to any terms in contracts with consumers. They therefore cover not only unfair exemption clauses, but also any other type of clause considered to be unfair. A consumer is defined in Regulation 3(1) as 'any natural person...acting for purposes which are outside his trade, business or profession'. The regulations apply to terms that have not been individually negotiated (Regulation 5(1)), but they do not apply (Regulation 6(2)) to terms defining the main subject matter of the contract, or to the adequacy of the price or remuneration for goods or services provided.

Regulation 5(1) states that a term will be regarded as unfair if, 'contrary to the requirement of good faith, it causes a significant imbalance...to the detriment of the consumer'. The unfairness of a term is to be assessed under Regulation 6(1) by taking into account the nature of the goods or services, the circumstances under which the contract was made and any other contractual terms on which it is dependent. For a term to be unfair, the significant imbalance it creates must be contrary to good faith. Parties are required to deal with each other in an open and honest way, taking into account their relative bargaining strengths.

- **Contract terms:** these are statements incorporated in the contract.
- **Conditions** go to the root of the contract and result in repudiation of the contract. **Warranties** are less important terms and give rise only to damages. **Innominate terms** are more flexible and can be treated as either conditions or warranties.
- **Express terms** are those things specifically agreed.
- **Implied terms** are those added by the law. The most important implied terms are those added

by statute under the **Sale of Goods Act 1979** and the **Supply of Goods and Services Act 1982**. Specific statutory remedies are available for breaches of these terms.
- **Exemption clauses** seek to exclude or limit liability. Common law controls require the clause to be incorporated in the contract and drawn to the attention of the other party. **Unfair Contract Terms Act 1977** and **Unfair Terms in Consumer Contracts Regulations 1999** regulate exemption clauses in consumer contracts.

Misrepresentation

Misrepresentation is a **vitiating factor**. This means it has the effect of invalidating consent. A contract may be declared void on grounds of misrepresentation (which may be fraudulent, negligent or innocent). A misrepresentation is an untrue statement of fact that induces a party to enter a contract but is not itself part of the contract.

Statement of fact

To avoid a contract, misrepresentation does not have to be verbal. Conduct may be sufficient, for example payment by cheque if the payer knows that his or her bank will not honour the cheque. Lord Campbell LC in *Walters* v *Morgan* (1861) referred to 'a nod, a wink, a shake of the head or a smile' qualifying as statements. The general rule is that silence as to relevant facts does not amount to misrepresentation — there is no liability for failing to disclose them to the other party. In *Peek* v *Gurney* (1873), Lord Cairns stated: 'Mere non-disclosure of material facts, however morally censurable, would form no ground for an action for misrepresentation.' However, if a party makes any representation on a particular matter, it must be full and frank — silence may not be used to distort a positive representation. A half-true statement, which is accurate as far as it goes but conveys a misleading impression by being incomplete, may give rise to a misrepresentation, as in *Dimmock* v *Hallett* (1866) and *Spice Girls Ltd* v *Aprilia* (2000). With contracts that demand *uberrima fides* (utmost good faith) — for example insurance contracts — parties are bound to disclose all material facts, whether or not they are asked about them.

A misrepresentation must be distinguished from a mere commendation, a statement of opinion (see the 1927 case of *Bisset* v *Wilkinson*) and a statement of future intention, but note that a statement of future intention can become a misrepresentation if, as in *Edgington* v *Fitzmaurice* (1885), it is proved that there was no intention to do the promised act at the time the statement was made.

Inducing a party to enter a contract

For misrepresentation to be proved, it must be shown that the relevant statement induced the party who is now complaining to enter the contract. This is particularly important where the party to whom the statement was made was in a position to check its truth for himself or herself; see *Attwood* v *Small* (1838). The misrepresentation does not have to be the only reason why the other party entered the contract, but there must be reliance on the statement.

Types of misrepresentation

Fraudulent misrepresentation

Fraudulent misrepresentation occurs when a party makes a false statement without honestly believing it to be true. It may be a deliberate lie, or it may be a statement made recklessly. The classic definition outlined by the House of Lords in *Derry* v *Peek* (1889) is a false statement made 'without belief in its truth, or recklessly as to whether it is true or false'.

Negligent misrepresentation

Following the rule in *Hedley Byrne* v *Heller* (1964), success when claiming negligent misrepresentation depends upon proof of a special relationship existing between the parties. The principle of liability is based on the duty of care in tort. Section 2(1) of the **Misrepresentation Act 1967** provides that a non-fraudulent misrepresentation will be treated in the same way as a fraudulent one, unless the person making it 'proves that he had reasonable ground to believe and did believe up to the time the contract was made the facts represented were true'. The burden placed on the defendant by the 1967 Act to prove that it was reasonable to believe and that he or she did believe in the truth of the statements may be difficult to discharge, as was shown in *Howard Marine and Dredging Co.* v *Ogden and Sons* (1978).

Innocent misrepresentation

For a misrepresentation to have been made innocently, the person making it has to have an honest belief in its truth, for example where repeating inaccurate information supplied by someone else. Even in this case, it may be possible to bring an action in equity for rescission.

Remedies for misrepresentation

Rescission

This is an equitable remedy, which sets the contract aside and puts the parties back in the position they were in before the contract was made. It is available for all types of misrepresentation.

The injured party can rescind the contract by notifying the other party, or if this is not possible because of the behaviour of the other party, the injured party will need to take some reasonable action to indicate the intention to rescind; see *Car and Universal Finance* v *Caldwell* (1965).

Rescission will not be ordered where it is impossible to return the parties to their original pre-contract positions. This would most obviously happen where the subject matter of the contract has been used up or destroyed, as was the case in *Vigers* v *Pike* (1842). Rescission cannot be ordered where a third party has acquired rights under the contract, as in *White* v *Garden* (1851).

> **Examiner tip**
>
> When answering an exam question you first of all need to discuss whether there is a misrepresentation. If there is, then you will have to decide what type of misrepresentation it is. What sort it is will affect the remedy that is available. Do not assume it is fraudulent unless there is evidence of dishonesty.

> **Examiner tip**
>
> Statements making promises are a clue that the question wants you to consider misrepresentation. Remember that if the statement becomes incorporated in the contract it could also be treated as an express term.

Damages

The availability of damages for the three types of misrepresentation is as follows:

- In the case of a fraudulent misrepresentation, damages for the tort of deceit can be claimed.
- In the case of a negligent misrepresentation, damages can be claimed either for the tort of negligence — following *Hedley Byrne* v *Heller* (1964) and *Esso Petroleum* v *Marden* (1976) — or under s.2(1) of the **Misrepresentation Act 1967**.
- In the case of an innocent misrepresentation, there is no right to damages. But under s.2(2) of the **Misrepresentation Act 1967** the court has discretion, in the case of an innocent misrepresentation, to award damages where it refuses to allow rescission.

Damages are available in circumstances where rescission is not an adequate remedy, as when some kind of consequential loss has occurred, for example the failure of a cooling system with the resulting loss of foodstuffs in storage. Damages for misrepresentation are calculated on the same basis as they are in tort, with the aim of putting the parties back in the position they were in before the misrepresentation was made.

Exclusion of liability for misrepresentation

Section 3 of the **Misrepresentation Act 1967**, as amended by s.8 of the **Unfair Contract Terms Act 1977**, provides that terms that seek to exclude liability for a misrepresentation are valid only if reasonable.

Summary

A **misrepresentation** is an untrue statement of fact that induces the other party to enter a contract. There are three types:

- **fraudulent** — a false statement that the maker does not believe to be true
- **negligent** — under the **Misrepresentation Act 1967** treated in the same way as fraudulent

unless the maker had reasonable grounds to believe the statement was true

- **innocent** — made in honest belief of its truth

Remedies include:

- rescission — equitable remedy available for all types of misrepresentation — sets the contract aside
- damages

Discharge of contract

A contract can be discharged, i.e. come to an end, in a number of ways: performance, agreement, frustration or breach.

Performance

The law expects performance of the terms of a contract to be exact and complete, and both parties must carry out their obligations under the contract; see *Re Moore and Landauer* (1921) and *Cutter* v *Powell* (1795). However, the courts do recognise the idea of substantial performance, which is where the work is almost completed and any minor defects can easily be corrected. In practice, therefore, it is a question of degree;

contrast *Hoenig* v *Isaacs* (1952) and *Bolton* v *Mahadeva* (1972). Partial performance is where some work has been done, but it is insufficient to amount to substantial performance. In *Sumpter* v *Hedges* (1898), a builder left houses and stables only half-constructed and the claimant had no choice but to have the work finished; this was, therefore, not partial performance. Completion by a third party is known as vicarious performance. The rule is that vicarious performance is acceptable in situations that are not of a personal nature, provided that all the other terms of the contract are met. Where personal, individual skills are involved, for example the painting of a portrait, vicarious performance is unlikely to be appropriate; see *Edwards* v *Newland* (1950).

Agreement

This occurs where a contract is abandoned or its terms are varied by agreement. Both parties enter into a new agreement and both must, therefore, provide consideration if the agreement is to be valid.

Frustration

This arises when an event occurs, during the lifetime of the contract, which is not the fault of either party and which makes completion of the contract:
- impossible, for example in *Morgan* v *Manser* (1948), and in *Taylor* v *Caldwell* (1863), where a music hall was hired for a series of concerts, but before the concert dates arrived, the hall was destroyed by fire
- illegal (perhaps due to a new statute or the outbreak of war)
- radically different (as when the postponement of the coronation of Edward VII meant that some contracts no longer had any point — contrast the 1903 cases of *Herne Bay Steamboat Co.* v *Hutton* and *Krell* v *Henry*)

Note that the substance of the agreement must be undermined — it is not sufficient that completion is made more difficult or expensive, and the courts have to determine whether the frustration is genuine; see *Davis Contractors* v *Fareham UDC* (1956). Also *Maritime National Fish* v *Ocean Trawlers* (1935) makes it clear that a party cannot rely on frustration which is wholly or partly self-induced. A contract that is frustrated comes to an end automatically as soon as the frustrating event occurs, and without further action by either party. All further obligations are then annulled, but the contract is not in itself void and past obligations generally remain in force. Section 1(2) of the **Law Reform (Frustrated Contracts) Act 1943** gives a right to recover money already paid under such a contract and to withhold anything still payable, and s.1(3) provides that, where a party has received some valuable benefit (other than the payment of money) under the contract before its discharge, the court may order him or her to make an appropriate payment to the other party. The court has discretion to try to do justice in a situation which is the fault of neither party and it can therefore mitigate the possible injustice of allowing the loss to remain where it has fallen.

Examiner tip

When discussing a contract which is frustrated, it is important to consider remedies and, in particular, the discretion that is allowed under the 1943 Act. Remember that the court would try to be fair to both parties, so all the facts in the question need to be considered when deciding what would be a fair outcome.

Knowledge check 38

What is the effect of frustration on a contract?

Breach

An actual breach is where there is a failure to fulfil an obligation under the contract or to fulfil it to the required standard; see the case of *Pilbrow* v *Pearless de Rougemont and Co.* (1999). Anticipatory breach occurs at some time before performance is due, when one party shows by express words or by implications from his or her conduct

that he or she does not intend to observe his or her obligations under the contract; this principle was established in *Hochster* v *De La Tour* (1853). The party injured by an anticipatory breach of contract has the option of waiting for the performance date to pass and then suing for breach; see *Avery* v *Bowden* (1855).

The effects of breach of contract

The rights of the injured party depend on the nature of the term broken. A breach of a condition is a breach of an important term, giving the right to terminate the agreement and repudiate (cancel) the contract. A breach of a warranty is a breach of a minor term, which does not go to the root of the contract, and gives rise only to a claim for damages. Where the breach is of an innominate term in a contract, if the results are so serious as to undermine the very foundation of the contract, the innocent party has the right to terminate the contract. The contract is not automatically ended by the breach, as the innocent party can choose whether to treat the contract as discharged or opt to continue with it.

An injured party may not always be able to insist on affirming the contract because, under the principle of mitigation of loss, the injured party usually has a general duty to take reasonable steps to minimise his loss. There are three rules on mitigation:

(1) A claimant cannot recover for loss that could have been avoided by taking reasonable steps.

(2) A claimant cannot recover for any loss that has actually been avoided, even if he or she went further than was necessary in compliance with the above rule.

(3) A claimant may recover extra loss incurred in taking reasonable but unsuccessful steps to mitigate loss.

In *British Westinghouse* v *Underground Electric Railways Co. of London* (1912), it was said that a claimant mitigating loss would not be expected to 'take any step which a reasonable and prudent man would not ordinarily take in the course of his business'.

Remedies for breach of contract

Damages

The purpose of damages, as stated in *Robinson* v *Harman* (1848), is that 'when a party sustains loss by reason of a breach of contract he is, so far as money can do it, to be placed in the same situation with respect to damages as if the contract had been performed'. For damages to be awarded, there must be a causal link between the breach of contract and the damage suffered, and this is a question of fact in each case. The courts have to decide how far the losses suffered by the injured party should be recoverable. The principle used is that losses are recoverable if they are reasonably within the contemplation of the parties as a probable result of the breach. This principle is known as the rule in *Hadley* v *Baxendale* (1854). The application of the principle is illustrated by the case of *Victoria Laundry* v *Newman Industries* (1949).

Sometimes the parties agree in advance what would be reasonable compensation in the event of a breach, and this is referred to as **liquidated damages**. The courts will accept this sum only if it represents an accurate and proper assessment of loss. If not, it will be treated as a 'penalty' and be unenforceable; see *Dunlop Pneumatic Tyre Co.* v *New Garage and Motor Co.* (1915).

Examiner tip

Damages will always be available as a remedy when there is a breach of contract, but note that the right to terminate the contract is also available when there is a breach of condition or a breach of a significant innominate term.

Damages that have not been agreed to in advance are known as **unliquidated damages**, and they will be determined by the court. Courts can award:

- **substantial damages** (a sum designed to compensate for actual losses suffered, which is the usual basis on which damages are calculated)
- **nominal damages** (a small sum, indicating that, although technically the party has a claim, the court does not feel that actual compensation is appropriate; see the 1830 case of *Staniforth* v *Lyall*)
- **exemplary damages** (a much larger sum than would be needed to compensate the injured party, to demonstrate the court's disapproval of the party at fault)

Because the aim of damages is to put the injured party as far as possible in the position he or she would have been in if the contract had been performed properly, damages are assessed depending on the circumstances of the case. The sum awarded may be based on the difference in value between the goods or services contracted for and the value of those actually delivered, or on the difference between the contract price and the market price if goods have to be obtained or sold elsewhere. In certain circumstances, damages may be awarded for intangible loss such as mental distress. In *Cook* v *Spanish Holiday Tours* (1960), damages for loss of enjoyment were paid to a honeymoon couple who were left without a room on their wedding night.

Knowledge check 39

What is the purpose of damages?

Equitable remedies

Unlike damages, the equitable remedies of injunction and specific performance are discretionary and are awarded by the court only if the circumstances of the case warrant it. Their use is appropriate when the award of damages would be inadequate and unjust. An injunction may also be an appropriate remedy to prevent someone from acting in breach of contract, for example by enforcing a contract in restraint of trade or a provision protecting trade secrets or specialist information.

'Specific performance' is an order of the court to make a party carry out his or her obligations under a contract, but it is appropriate only in situations where the subject matter of the contract is unique in some way, as in *Falcke* v *Gray* (1859), where the contract concerned a valuable work of art.

Summary

Performance — the law expects all terms of a contract to be complied with.

Frustration — this arises when an event occurs which is not the fault of either party. The **Law Reform (Frustrated Contracts) Act 1943** provides for equitable sharing of losses, e.g. return of monies paid.

Breach of contract — failure to perform an obligation under the contract:
- breach of condition — breach of an important term — innocent party can repudiate the contract
- breach of warranty — breach of minor term — innocent party can only sue for damages
- actual breach

- anticipatory breach — innocent party does not have to wait for actual breach, but can treat contract as at an end and sue for damages

Damages is the remedy for all types of breach:
- liquidated — where parties have agreed in advance what the damages should be in the event of a breach
- unliquidated — will be determined by the court
- it must be clear that the breach of contract has caused the damage
- damages must not be too remote
- the claimant has a duty to mitigate his or her loss

Equitable remedies — injunction and specific performance are discretionary remedies.

Critical evaluation of contract law

In this examination paper, Question 3 requires students to evaluate how effectively the law operates. This question needs to be approached in a different way from the other two parts. It is important to plan in advance the kind of comments that you intend to make and then adapt them to suit the actual question that is asked. Questions will either be on formation of contract (general or specifically on offer and acceptance), contract terms (general or specifically on exemption clauses) or remedies.

Formation of contract

Offer and acceptance

In some situations, it is difficult to determine what constitutes an offer. The case of *Clarke* v *Dunraven* (1897), for example, does not seem to fit with the conventional idea of offer and acceptance. In that case, entering a yacht race created a contract between all the competitors. The House of Lords agreed that there was a contract, yet there was no specific offer and acceptance between individual competitors.

Are the rules that distinguish offers from invitations satisfactory? A good answer will briefly outline the relevant rules and comment on them. Are the cases decided appropriately? Probably most people will agree that the rules on self-service stores are sensible, but what about the outcome of *Fisher* v *Bell*? There is still some confusion in deciding whether some things, such as timetables and tickets for transport, are offers or invitations to treat. Another issue is the difficulty in distinguishing between counter-offers and requests for information. Refer back to the rules and decide whether you think they are sufficiently clear.

Because in unilateral contracts acceptance can be through conduct, it may not always be clear when performance that amounts to acceptance has started. Arguably, it would be unfair in many situations to allow acceptance to be valid from the first act. For example, looking for a lost item but not finding it would not be performance, but perhaps, once it is found, even if not yet returned, performance has begun. Equally, it would be unfair for an offeror to revoke his or her offer when the offeree has already done a substantial amount of work in response to it. The Law Commission in 1975 declared that an offer which the offeror has said will be open for a specific period should not be revocable within that time.

Is the 'postal rule' appropriate in view of the other means of communication available in the twenty-first century? A person accepting an offer can easily check whether any e-mailed acceptance has been received, possibly using another instantaneous method of communication, such as the telephone. Even when letter post is delivered, it is still possible that letters opened in the front office may not be seen by an intended recipient until much later.

Because some modern methods of communication are considered to be instantaneous, other problems arise. In the *Entores* case, Denning LJ suggested that the burden should rest with the person accepting an offer to make sure his or her communication has been received. For example, if the telephone goes dead, there is a need to telephone again. This approach was approved by the House of Lords in the

AQA A2 Law

Brinkibon case, and it does seem reasonable to put the onus on the person accepting to check that the acceptance has been received.

The case law on standard form contracts demonstrates the courts' problems in deciding what is offer and what is acceptance. It could be argued that the whole situation created by businesses using their own standard terms is unsatisfactory. The judgement in *Butler Machine Tool Co.* v *Ex-Cell-O Corporation* (1979) highlights the difficulty in identifying precisely whose terms the contract is actually based on when there is a 'battle of the forms'.

Reform

No comprehensive proposals for reform have been made. This is an area of law where Parliament has not found it necessary to intervene because the courts have been able to adapt the existing rules to suit changing circumstances. An increasing number of contracts are made electronically and many of the older rules are likely to be redundant. There are currently European regulations that apply to website contracting, but they specifically exclude contracts made by exchange of e-mails. In view of the complexity and importance of this area, further EU directives are likely to be the source of reforms in the future.

Consideration

A number of questions need to be considered. Is it fair that something that is not market value can be good consideration? Is it helpful to have a distinction between sufficiency and adequacy? The courts are not interested in whether it is a good or a bad bargain, but simply in whether a bargain exists. Have the rules on past consideration worked fairly? Cases such as *Re McArdle* and *Re Casey's Patents* could be discussed here.

In respect of existing duty rules, the 1990 case of *Williams* v *Roffey* shows that the courts are making real efforts to consider the commercial reality of the situations facing parties in commercial contracts. It seems unlikely, however, following cases such as *Re Selectmove* (1995), that this development will be taken any further.

There is also a problem with promises to accept part-payment of debts. The rule that, without consideration, a promise to accept part-payment is not binding was criticised by the Court of Appeal in *Couldery* v *Bartrum* (1881). Nevertheless, it can be argued in defence of the rule that it protects creditors who are in a weak bargaining position from being forced into accepting less than they are owed.

Both the case of *Williams* v *Roffey* and the law of promissory estoppel (expounded by Denning J in the 1947 case of *Central London Property Trust* v *High Trees House Ltd*) seem to be an attack on the doctrine of consideration, but Professor Atiyah has suggested that if offer, acceptance and intention to create legal relations are all in place, then there is no need for consideration. Promissory estoppel (the principle that if a promisor makes a promise, which another person acts on, the promisor is stopped from breaking the promise, even if the other party did not provide consideration) seems a fair solution to the problem of promises to accept part-payment of debts. However, it is subject to many conditions (for example Birkett LJ said in *Combe* v *Combe* (1951) that it should be 'used as a shield and not as a sword'), and there is some uncertainty about aspects of it.

Examiner tip

If a question asks about formation of contract issues, you should try to discuss consideration or intention to create legal relations, as well as offer and acceptance.

Reform

It remains true that a requirement for consideration allows parties who make promises to escape liability. At the end of the eighteenth century, Lord Mansfield argued that a moral obligation could amount to consideration, but this view was firmly overruled in *Eastwood* v *Kenyon* in 1840. In 1937, the Law Revision Committee proposed reforms to the use of consideration. It suggested that:

- a written promise should always be binding, with or without consideration
- past consideration should be valid
- performance of an existing duty should be good consideration
- a creditor should be bound by a promise to accept part-payment in full settlement of a debt

To date none of these proposals has been adopted.

One reform that has been made is the change introduced by the **Contracts (Rights of Third Parties) Act 1999** affecting third parties who are beneficiaries of contracts — they can now enforce them, even though they have supplied no consideration (see above). This means that cases like *Tweddle* v *Atkinson* would probably be decided differently today.

Examiner tip

Note that questions will require some discussion of possible reforms.

Intention to create legal relations

Relatively few problems that come before the courts are specifically related to the intention to create legal relations. One reason for this is that many of the situations where it might be relevant are domestic or social so that, often, there is no consideration. It could be argued that there is no need for a separate requirement of intention to create legal relations and that, provided there is valid offer and acceptance, and consideration is present, there is no reason in law why the agreement should not be valid. Feminists have argued that the requirement serves to reinforce the stereotype of the woman in the home not contributing anything of economic value.

A further point that could be made is that the 'binding in honour' exception for football pools agreements does not seem to be justified and can result in unfairness in cases like *Jones* v *Vernons Pools*.

Contract terms

One point that can be made is that the distinction between conditions and warranties is arguably fair because of the emphasis on the relative importance of the term in question. The contrast between the situations in *Bettini* v *Gye* and *Poussard* v *Spiers* would seem to justify treating the terms in different ways.

The issue of innominate terms can also be considered. Does the idea of having terms that vary in effect create welcome flexibility or create confusion? The idea clouds the distinction between conditions and warranties and yet it recognises the reality of what parties do in practice and enables the courts to deal with each case on its merits. On the other hand, if terms were fixed in their effect, there would be the advantage of certainty.

The implied terms in the **Sale of Goods Act 1979** and the **Supply of Goods and Services Act 1982** provide important safeguards for consumers, but do the provisions work in a sensible way? Look particularly at the cases dealing with description of goods. Have the courts applied the right balance when interpreting the statutes? Think about the decisions in *Reardon Smith Line* v *Hansen-Tangen*, *Clegg* v *Anderson* (2003) and *Bramhill* v *Edwards*.

Note that the **Supply of Goods and Services Act 1982** provided protection for those hiring goods, and extended the **Sale of Goods Act 1979** implied terms to goods supplied as part of a service, as well as introducing specific terms in respect of services. These are important additions to the rights of consumers. But have the changes made by the **Sale and Supply of Goods Act 1994** improved the protection given to consumers? Section 1(2) states: 'Where the seller sells goods in the course of a business, there is an implied term that the goods supplied under the contract are of satisfactory quality.' This is certainly more easily understood by consumers than was the 'merchantable quality' of which the **Sale of Goods Act 1979** spoke. The 1994 Act also adds some clarification on the meaning of 'satisfactory'.

Acceptance of goods

One significant criticism of the **Sale of Goods Act 1979** was over the issue of acceptance, but s.2(6) of the **Sale and Supply of Goods Act 1994** has since modified the law, stating that the buyer must have a reasonable opportunity to examine goods and that even having something repaired may not amount to acceptance. It seems that simply signing a receipt to acknowledge delivery does not amount to acceptance. However, the courts do not appear to have been entirely consistent in the way they have treated acceptance. Compare *Bernstein* v *Pamson Motors* with *Rogers* v *Parish (Scarborough)*.

Freedom of contract

Is it right that the law should interfere with what the parties have freely contracted to do? Most commentators accept that the protection afforded to consumers is necessary. The original Sale of Goods Act was passed in 1893, at a time when freedom of contract was more of a sacred doctrine than it is today, and the provisions of that original statute were based on rules that had been developed by the common law. Note the current distinction between business and private sales. Is the law right to treat these differently?

Exemption clauses

Look at the common law's treatment of exemption clauses. The emphasis is on incorporation and interpretation, rather than on the clauses' actual merits. Note, however, Denning LJ's effort in *Spurling* v *Bradshaw* to address more fundamental concerns with the 'red hand' rule. The **Unfair Contract Terms Act 1977** seems to have been successful in addressing the issues that the common law was unable to deal with. In particular, it introduced the idea of the consumer sale, allowing the law to offer specific protection to the most vulnerable. It also deals with standard form contracts. But does the Act strike the right balance?

Examiner tip

In an evaluation question on contract terms in general, mark schemes are likely to allow a variety of approaches. One approach might be to evaluate terms in general, e.g. express and implied terms, descriptions of terms as conditions, warranties and innominate terms. Another might be to focus on specific kinds of terms, e.g. statutory implied terms. A third approach would be an evaluation of terms excluding or limiting liability.

Overlap between the Unfair Contract Terms Act 1977 and the Unfair Terms in Consumer Contracts Regulations 1999

This is an important area to consider. Note that the 1999 Regulations originate from an EU directive and, although they overlap with the provisions of the 1977 Act in some respects, they are wider because they do not just apply to exclusion and limitation clauses. They are narrower, however, in that they apply only to consumer contacts where the terms are not individually negotiated. Because the Regulations and the Act overlap, there is the danger of confusion, especially as the test of unfairness in the Regulations is different from the approach in the Act. The Law Commission report, *Unfair Terms in Contracts* (2005), recommended the introduction of a single Act, replacing the Regulations and the 1977 Act. It also recommended extending to small businesses (in certain circumstances) the protection currently offered to consumers.

Examiner tip

A question on contract terms does not require discussion of formation of contract and mark schemes would not allow this to be credited.

Remedies

Damages are always available as a remedy for all kinds of breach of contract. They are the usual remedy and available as of right where a contract is breached. In many cases it is possible for an award of damages to place the claimant in the same situation as if the contract had been performed. The requirements that the defendant must have caused the breach, that the loss must not be too remote and that the claimant must mitigate his or her loss appear reasonable and ensure fairness between the parties. Damages would usually be a satisfactory remedy in contract cases because it is likely that an appropriate sum of money will put the claimant in the same position as if the contract had been properly carried out. Occasionally though damages will not be sufficient — for example, when the contract relates to something unique like a work of art, as in *Falcke* v *Gray* (1859) — and here it is useful to have the additional equitable remedy of specific performance.

There is also the issue that the rule in *Hadley* v *Baxendale* means that only losses which are within the contemplation of the parties can be claimed. This could result, as it did in *Victoria Laundries* v *Newman,* in a claimant suffering loss as a result of breach that they cannot recover. When losses are apportioned for frustrated contracts, it is possible to achieve a fair balance between the parties. However, this is not available for breach. The Law Commission has indicated that there should be provision for apportioning losses more fairly, similar to that for contributory negligence.

Unlike damages, equitable remedies are discretionary and will be awarded by the court only if the circumstances of the case warrant their use. For example, an injunction may be an appropriate remedy to prevent someone from acting in breach of contract, by enforcing a contract in restraint of trade or a provision protecting trade secrets or specialist information. However, this remedy is available in a fairly limited range of circumstances.

The remedy of rescission is equitable and therefore discretionary, but it is available for all types of misrepresentation. But rescission will not be ordered where it is impossible to return the parties to their original pre-contract positions. This would most obviously happen where the subject matter of the contract has been used up or destroyed, as was the case in *Vigers* v *Pike* (1842). This does seem reasonable as does the rule that rescission cannot be ordered where a third party has acquired rights under the contract, as in *White* v *Garden* (1851).

Before 1964, the only remedy for non-fraudulent misrepresentation was rescission. Damages were not available unless fraud could be proved. This situation was unsatisfactory and was changed by the decision in *Hedley Byrne* (1964), a tort case, and by the **Misrepresentation Act 1967**, which provides a specific remedy of damages, where a remedy would have been available if the misrepresentation had been fraudulent. This reform means that claimants who have suffered non-fraudulent misrepresentation are provided with the simple remedy of damages rather than having to use rescission and end the contract.

Breach of implied terms

The remedies available for breach of implied terms have been strengthened for consumers by the **Sale and Supply of Goods to Consumers Regulations 2002**. Under these regulations, consumers have additional remedies available: repair or replacement of the goods and a partial or full refund. One issue is that a right to reject is lost once the goods have been accepted and the claim would then be limited to damages, which in some situations, for example where the product had malfunctioned several times, would not be as attractive. However, damages may be more appropriate than rejection when supplies of a product are limited and buying an alternative is difficult, or where consumers have suffered personal injury because of a faulty product and wish to sue for consequential loss. The consumer will often be awarded sums far exceeding the value of the product itself, as in *Grant* v *Australian Knitting Mills* (1936) and *Godley* v *Perry* (1960). Another circumstance where damages may be appropriate is where the consumer has lost the right to reject by virtue of accepting the product.

The range of remedies available in contract law does seem to be adequate and there are no proposals for substantial reform.

Formation of contract

Issues of offer and acceptance:
- offers and invitations
- unilateral contracts
- postal rule and modern methods of communication
- reform

Consideration issues:
- market value
- existing duty
- part payment of debts
- promissory estoppel
- reform

Intention to create legal relations

Contract terms:
- issues with conditions, warranties and innominate terms
- issues with statutory implied terms
- issues with exemption clauses

Remedies:
- damages
- equitable remedies
- remedies for breaches of implied terms

Summary

Questions & Answers

How to use this section

This section of the guide provides you with questions that cover most of the Unit 3 topics. All the questions are followed by A-grade answers demonstrating both the structured technique that you should adopt and how to use case and statutory authorities effectively.

For 'problem-solving' questions based on a short scenario, the mnemonic **IDEA** may help you with planning and structuring your answers:

I **Identify** both the appropriate offence(s) and defence(s), or in the case of contract law the appropriate cause(s) of action and defence(s).

D **Define** the offence(s) and defence(s), or cause(s) of action and defence(s).

E **Explain** the various legal rules.

A **Apply** these rules to the facts of the question, using authorities (both cases and statutes) to support your answer.

Examiner's comments

Each question is followed by a brief analysis of what to watch out for when answering it (shown by the icon ⓔ). The student's answers are accompanied by examiner's comments (preceded by the icon ⓔ). These comments explain the elements of the answer for which marks can be awarded, show why high marks would be given and provide an insight into what examiners are looking for. You are strongly encouraged to download past papers and mark schemes from the AQA website (www.aqa.org.uk) or to obtain these from your teacher.

If you practise adapting the style of the A-grade answers to different question scenarios, it will enable you readily to identify the correct offences (or causes of action) and defences and then to structure your answer effectively using relevant cases and statutes.

Section A

Question 1 **Non-fatal offence against the person**

Darren and Michael are captains of opposing rugby teams with a history of 'bad blood' between them. These teams are drawn against each other in the semi-final of the regional rugby competition. During this match, Darren tackles Michael as he is about to score a try in injury time. However, the tackle is judged by the referee to be a high one and Darren is sent off the field. As a result of the tackle, Michael's collarbone is fractured and, in falling heavily to the ground, he also loses a tooth.

Discuss Darren's criminal liability for the injuries to Michael.   (25 marks)

Problem-solving questions based on a scenario require you to identify possible offences, to explain both *actus reus* and *mens rea* elements, and then to apply these to the facts stated. Relevant defences also need to be explained and applied.

A-grade answer

Given the nature of the injuries that Michael sustained, Darren could be charged with any of three offences under the Offences against the Person Act 1861: grievous bodily harm (GBH) under s.20, wounding (also under s.20) and assault occasioning actual bodily harm (ABH) under s.47. The loss of the tooth would normally be charged as a s.47 offence but, as bleeding would have been caused, this could equally be charged as wounding under s.20. Wounding was defined in the case of *JCC* v *Eisenhower* as a breach of both the inner and outer layers of skin.

For both wounding and infliction of GBH under s.20, the *mens rea* is now accepted as being intention or recklessness as to causing some harm, albeit not serious harm. This was established in the case of *R* v *Mowatt* and confirmed in the case of *R* v *Grimshaw*. It is, therefore, not necessary for the prosecution to seek to prove that the defendant intended GBH or wounding or was reckless as to whether he caused them or not.

In the present case, there can be no doubt that Darren directly caused Michael's injuries — both the 'but for' test for factual causation and the legal rules of causation are clearly satisfied, and it could be strongly argued that the high tackle was at least reckless in the *R* v *Cunningham* sense of 'conscious unjustified risk-taking'. If Darren were to be charged with s.47 assault occasioning ABH for the loss of the tooth, it would not be difficult to prove that this injury met the standard of ABH — 'any injury calculated to interfere with the health or comfort of the victim' (Miller), and the prosecution would only have to prove that Darren assaulted or battered Michael (inflicting unlawful personal violence), which self-evidently he did. The *mens rea* for s.47 is the same as for battery — intention or subjective recklessness as to the *actus reus* of battery. There is no need for the prosecution to establish that a defendant intended or was reckless as to causing ABH — this important rule was laid down by the House of Lords in the cases of *R v Savage* and *R v Parmenter* (both 1992), and was reaffirmed in *R v Roberts*. In the rugby match, the high tackle on Michael by Darren could certainly be described as reckless.

e The key elements of s.20 are clearly explained with effective use of relevant case authorities. The application is straightforward.

As to defences that Darren could plead, there would appear to be only one — that of consent. This is a limited defence and usually available only in respect of the minor crimes of assault and battery. For the more serious non-fatal offences — ABH and GBH — it can only be successfully pleaded if the activity out of which the injury arises is surgery, including tattooing or body-piercing; rough horseplay; or sport. It is this last category with which we are concerned here. The general rule in contact sports such as rugby is that players are presumed to have consented to serious injuries, provided these occur within the rules of the game. In this case, it is clear from the referee's decision in sending Darren off the field that the tackle constituted foul play; see *R v Billinghurst* where the defence of consent was allowed in the case of a rugby match. However, the Court of Appeal in *R v Barnes* ruled that criminal prosecutions should only be brought against a sportsperson if his or her conduct was grave enough to be properly categorised as criminal. In the present case, even given the severity of the injury, it is possible that a court would hold that Darren's conduct did not meet the threshold test for a successful prosecution, as high tackles are foreseeable in any rugby match.

e All the key rules of consent are explained — the reference to *Barnes* is particularly relevant here.

e **24/25 marks awarded.** This question is comprehensively and accurately answered. Sound use is made of relevant case authorities.

Question 2 GBH and involuntary manslaughter

Adrian and Brian were in a nightclub, where Adrian took some drugs. Shortly afterwards, Adrian began to act in a strange manner, giggling and stumbling about. When Adrian clumsily spilled a drink over Chris, Brian decided it was time to get him home. As they left the nightclub, they were followed by Chris and his friend Don. Chris challenged Adrian to a fight and Adrian took off his jacket and then immediately lashed out at Chris before Chris was prepared. The blow sent Chris reeling backwards and he dislocated his knee in a very awkward fall.

Meanwhile, Brian had run off but had been caught by Don in a disused building. Don was holding Brian tightly round the neck and causing him to choke, but Brian managed to elbow him twice in the face. Don released his grip, suddenly collapsed, and was sick as he lay on his back. Brian looked at him for a few seconds and then walked away. Don was later found to have died by choking on his vomit.

Adapted from AQA examination paper, June 2002

(a) Discuss Adrian's criminal liability in connection with the injury to Chris. (25 marks)

e As with all problem-solving questions, you need to explain and apply relevant *actus reus* and *mens rea* for appropriate offences, and then to consider what defences may be available.

(b) Discuss Brian's criminal liability for the involuntary manslaughter of Don. (25 marks)

e As with all problem-solving questions, you need to explain and apply the rules of both types of involuntary manslaughter.

A-grade answer

(a) In terms of the severity of the injury that Chris sustained — the dislocated knee — Adrian could face a charge under s.20 or s.18 of the Offences against the Person Act 1861.

Section 20 requires that the defendant caused GBH to the victim as the *actus reus* of this offence. Grievous bodily harm was defined as 'really serious harm' in *DPP* v *Smith* (1961), but this was revised to 'serious harm' in *R* v *Saunders* (1985). As the scenario states that 'Adrian…lashed out at Chris' and 'the blow sent Chris reeling', there would appear to be no difficulty in proving the necessary causation — under both the 'but for' and the legal rules of causation. There was no intervening act between the blow and the injury, and Adrian's action was certainly a 'significant contribution' to the dislocated knee; see *R* v *Cheshire* (1991).

e Having correctly identified that this injury would constitute GBH, the answer explains the *actus reus* and then applies it with effective use of case law.

The *mens rea* of a s.20 offence is now settled as either intention or recklessness to cause some harm. This was decided in *R* v *Mowatt* and confirmed in the case of *R* v *Grimshaw*. It is not, therefore, necessary for the Crown to prove that the defendant intended to cause GBH or was reckless as to whether this would be the outcome. Here, the circumstances clearly suggest that, in starting the fight by lashing out at Chris before he was prepared, Adrian intended to cause at least some harm to Chris.

e The *mens rea* of s.20 is accurately described and then straightforwardly applied.

The *actus reus* of s.18 is identical to that of s.20 — either wounding or GBH. The main difference between these two offences is that of *mens rea*. Section 18 is defined as an offence of specific intent, so to secure a conviction, the Crown must prove that the defendant intended to cause GBH. Intention can be direct (where the defendant had the aim or purpose of causing GBH) or oblique (where the defendant's intent is sufficient if the jury decide he or she foresaw the outcome of GBH as 'virtually certain', as in the cases of *R* v *Nedrick* and *R* v *Woollin*). In this case, even if Adrian could argue he did not wish the actual outcome, nonetheless it is certainly possible for him to be convicted of a s.18 offence, as the action of striking another person so hard that he or she reels backwards and falls could be viewed by the jury as coming within the test laid down in the *Nedrick* and *Woollin* cases. In a case such as Adrian's, where no weapon has been used, it is more usual for the Crown to prosecute on the basis of a s.20 charge.

e This is a very effective paragraph dealing with s.18, with oblique intent clearly explained and applied.

The defences open to Adrian are limited. It is a clear rule of law that consent cannot be pleaded to ordinary fighting (*R* v *Donovan*), still less to an incident that has resulted in GBH. If he is charged under s.20, Adrian cannot use the defence of intoxication. The cases of *DPP* v *Majewski* and *R* v *Lipman* confirm that voluntary intoxication by drink or drugs can only be pleaded as a partial defence to crimes of specific intent. Section 20 is a basic-intent crime. The defence of automatism, which, if successful, negates the *actus reus* of an offence, is also problematic for Adrian. This defence requires the defendant to prove that, at the time he or she committed the offence, he or she was not in control of his or her actions. Here again, Adrian would face legal difficulties because, for clear policy reasons, the courts are unwilling to allow such a defence if the loss of control has been caused by voluntary intoxication by alcohol or illegal drugs. It is also arguably correct that Adrian was in control of his actions when he attacked Chris because, before doing so, he carefully removed his jacket.

e The defence of consent is justifiably rejected, but the issue of intoxication is dealt with more fully.

e 24 or 25/25 marks awarded.

(b) Involuntary manslaughter is defined as unlawful killing without malice aforethought, which is intention to kill or commit GBH. It can be committed in two different ways — by an unlawful and dangerous act or by gross negligence. The former requires a positive act, which in this case this would be the blows that Brian struck with his elbow; gross negligence is committed by an omission, which would be Brian's walking away from Don, who was clearly distressed.

ⓔ This is a clear opening section which defines involuntary manslaughter and identifies (with reasons) which type would be relevant here.

Unlawful and dangerous act manslaughter, also referred to as constructive or Church doctrine manslaughter, first of all requires that the defendant has committed a crime — the unlawful act cannot be a tort or contract (*R v Franklin*). By striking Don with his elbows and causing him to collapse, it can be argued that Brian could have committed GBH, and certainly ABH. The *mens rea* for manslaughter is the *mens rea* of the unlawful act; if the charge was s.47 ABH or s.20 GBH, the *mens rea* would be either intention or Cunningham recklessness (conscious taking of an unjustified risk). As the blows by Brian must have been struck with the intent of causing at least some harm to Don, the *mens rea* requirement of both offences s.47 and s.20 is satisfied, and accordingly Brian has the necessary *mens rea* for manslaughter.

The second requirement is that the unlawful act must also be dangerous. In *Church* (confirmed by *DPP v Newbury and Jones*), this was defined as 'dangerous in the sense that a sober and reasonable person would recognise that the act carried the risk of some harm albeit not serious injury'. The use of an elbow to strike the victim twice in the face would certainly satisfy this limited test.

The final test is that the unlawful act must have caused the death of the victim (*R v Goodfellow*). Here, Brian's attack satisfies both the factual 'but for' test of causation and the legal rules established in *R v Smith* and *R v Cheshire*. His attack was both the substantial and operating cause of death and a significant contribution to Don's death.

It can therefore be strongly argued that Brian has both the *actus reus* and *mens rea* of unlawful and dangerous act manslaughter.

ⓔ All elements of unlawful act manslaughter are correctly explained with effective application.

In respect of his omission in walking away from Don, who was clearly seriously ill having collapsed and been sick, Brian could be liable for manslaughter by gross negligence. This is based on the civil tort of negligence and requires there to be a duty of care, the breach of which causes the victim's death, and gross negligence that the jury believes makes the act criminal and thus deserving of punishment. The issue of duty of care relies on the incremental tests established in *Caparo v Dickman* — foreseeability of harm, proximity and the policy test of whether it is fair, just and reasonable to impose a duty of care. Here, it could be argued that having struck Don and caused his collapse, the reasonable person would foresee some further harm, and there is clearly proximity in terms of time and space. There is also no policy reason why a duty should not be imposed. It could also be alleged that by walking away in these circumstances, Brian breached his duty of care — this test is also an objective test based on the 'reasonable man'. The issue of causation has already been addressed above.

The final issue, that of gross negligence itself, is one for the jury to decide upon. In the leading case of *Adomako*, Lord Mackay declined to define what gross negligence meant, choosing to leave this to the jury as he felt that such a definition would be incomprehensible. However, in *R v Singh*, the trial judge laid down the following test for the jury: 'The question posed is having regard to the risk of death involved, was the defendant's conduct so bad in all the circumstances as to amount in your judgement to a criminal act or omission?' This direction was later approved by the Court of Appeal.

Lord Taylor CJ in *Adomako* had suggested that 'inattention or failure to address a serious risk which goes beyond mere carelessness in respect of an obvious matter which the defendant's duty demanded he should address' could properly lead a jury to make a finding of gross negligence.

In the light of these legal rulings, Brian could be convicted of gross negligence manslaughter, but it remains much more likely on the facts of this case that he would be convicted of unlawful and dangerous act manslaughter.

ⓔ Again, all elements of gross negligence manslaughter are both explained and applied. The concluding sentence confirms this is a sound answer.

In his defence, Brian could plead self-defence. It is the position under both common law and statute — s.3 of the Criminal Law Act 1967 — that a person if attacked is entitled to protect himself by using such force as is reasonable in all the circumstances. Where justified, this can provide a complete defence by negating the unlawfulness of the homicide or assault — in effect, this defence renders the circumstances that surround the act not unlawful. Given that Don 'was holding Brian tightly round the neck and causing him to choke', it could be argued that Brian's reaction of elbowing him twice in the face was both a proportionate and reasonable use of force.

ⓔ Self-defence is dealt with in a straightforward way, and this section would certainly qualify as 'strong clear'.

ⓔ **24/25 marks awarded.**

Question 3 Murder, loss of self-control and diminished responsibility

Fred became annoyed by the late-night parties being held by his neighbour, Gemma, and he sent her a threatening text message. This was read by Gemma's daughter, Hannah, who became very worried about it. When Hannah told Gemma, Gemma went round to Fred's house and a furious argument broke out, during which Gemma attacked Fred, causing serious injuries.

A few days later, Fred's son, John, saw Gemma's boyfriend, Keiran, in a café. Keiran laughed and made a loud remark about Fred being beaten up by a woman. He also shouted that John was a 'complete alcoholic nutter'. Because of his prolonged abuse of drink and drugs, John was prone to irrational, aggressive responses to various situations. He picked up a knife from a table and stabbed Keiran in the body. Keiran thought that he had simply been punched and did not at first seek medical treatment. When he finally went to the Accident and Emergency department at the hospital, he was thought to be a low priority case and was not immediately dealt with. By the time the mistake was discovered, it was too late to save Keiran's life.

Adapted from AQA examination paper, June 2009

Discuss the criminal liability of John for the murder of Keiran.   (25 marks)

ⓔ This problem-solving question requires both explanation of all relevant offence components — *actus reus* and *mens rea* of murder — together with relevant defences — in this case, loss of self-control and diminished responsibility.

A-grade answer

Murder is defined as unlawful killing with malice aforethought where the *actus reus* is the unlawful killing and the *mens rea* — malice aforethought — means intention either to kill or to commit grievous bodily harm. As murder is a result crime, the prosecution must prove that the actions of the defendant were the factual and legal cause of the victim's death. In this case, John's action in stabbing Keiran was certainly the factual cause of death as 'but for' that action, Keiran would not have died. However, there is a problem with legal rules of causation. These state that the defendant's action need not be the only cause of death but must have been the 'substantive and operating cause of death' as in *R* v *Smith*. Because Keiran failed to recognise he had been stabbed and not simply punched, he did not immediately seek medical attention. This would give John the opportunity to argue that this failure effectively broke the causal chain, especially if medical evidence supported the view that prompt medical attention would have prevented Keiran's death. The prosecution would, however, argue that the stab wound remained the operative cause of death and that it was foreseeable that Keiran might not seek immediate treatment. Following from *R* v *Roberts*, a further prosecution argument would be that such a mistake by Keiran was 'not daft' so there was no break in the causal chain. The issue

of possible medical negligence in giving Keiran's case a low priority would not of itself break the causal chain as this negligence did not appear to reach the required threshold of being 'palpably wrong'.

(e) Murder is clearly defined and the causation issues are comprehensively explained and applied. So far this is a sound answer.

The *mens rea* for murder is intention to kill (express malice) or commit grievous bodily harm (implied malice) — *R* v *Vickers*. In this case, it could be argued that when he stabbed Keiran with a knife, John must at least have intended to cause GBH which is sufficient for murder. There is no need to consider the oblique intent rule — defendant's foresight of virtually certain consequences.

However, as partial defences to the murder charge, John could plead loss of self-control under ss.54–56 of the Coroners and Justice Act 2009 and diminished responsibility (s.2) under the Homicide Act 1957 as amended by the 2009 Act.

Loss of self-control requires the defendant to prove that his actions in killing Keiran resulted from a loss of self-control, which had a qualifying trigger, and a person of the defendant's sex and age, with a normal degree of tolerance and self-restraint and in the circumstances of the defendant, might have reacted in the same or in a similar way to the defendant. The qualifying trigger here would be the anger trigger: 'things done or said which— (a) constituted circumstances of an extremely grave character, and (b) caused D to have a justifiable sense of being seriously wronged'.

Assuming he could establish that he had lost self-control, John would have to prove that this was caused by the 'loud remark about Fred being beaten up by a woman' which Keiran uttered, and that these words satisfied the above two tests. These tests are objective and on the face of it, the initial words spoken by Kieran could not be viewed as 'circumstances of an extremely grave character' which then 'caused D to have a justifiable sense of being seriously wronged'. However, the further shout — 'complete alcoholic nutter' — could be regarded as meeting both these tests as it could be argued that the word 'circumstances' in the first test could not ignore the defendant's circumstances since Keiran's shout directly focused on his 'prolonged abuse of drink and drugs'.

These particular circumstances would also have to be considered in the final objective test — whether a person of the defendant's sex and age, with a normal degree of tolerance and self-restraint and in the circumstances of the defendant, might have reacted in the same way as the defendant. In *A-G for Jersey* v *Holley*, the House of Lords held that where a defendant suffered from a psychological condition, the preferred defence should be diminished responsibility unless the provocative words were specifically directed at the defendant's mental condition, which was the case here. The jury would therefore be directed to consider the gravity of this last remark on the normal person in the same circumstances as John, and whether that normal person would then have reacted as John did in losing self-control and killing Keiran.

(e) All elements in the loss of self-control defence are explained — especially the issue of the qualifying trigger and the objective test, which correctly includes the ruling from *Holley*. This is a sound response.

John could also plead diminished responsibility under the revised s.2 Homicide Act 1957 which requires the defendant to prove, on the balance of probabilities, that he or she was suffering from an abnormality of mental functioning which arose from a recognised medical condition and which substantially impaired the defendant's ability to understand the nature of his or her conduct or to form a rational judgement or to exercise self-control. Because of his 'irrational, aggressive responses', it could certainly be argued John suffered from an abnormality of mental functioning. Expert psychiatric evidence would then be needed to establish that this arose from a recognised medical condition. In the case of *R* v *Tandy*, it was held that for drink (and drugs) to produce an abnormality of mind, they would have had to have reached such a level as to cause brain damage. If this is proved here, it is likely that this defence would succeed as this condition would probably satisfy the final test — that the abnormality of mental functioning substantially impaired John's ability to form a rational judgement or to exercise self-control.

(e) This is another sound answer on this defence — the section dealing with the drink and drug abuse is effectively explained and applied with the appropriate case authority.

(e) **24 or 25/25 marks awarded.**

Question 4 **Critical evaluation of law on non-fatal offences**

Critically analyse the present law on non-fatal offences and suggest possible reforms. (25 marks)

(e) Evaluative questions are answered most effectively by explaining the weaknesses and problems in the present law, although it is possible to obtain marks by indicating how the existing law may be satisfactory. Usually such questions also require some ideas for possible reform — these should be based on Law Commission proposals if possible.

A-grade answer

The first observation to be made about the law on non-fatal offences is that it is not completely codified. The separate offences of assault and battery remain common law offences, albeit with their separate nature confirmed in s.39 of the Criminal Justice Act 1988, but the more serious offences — assault occasioning actual bodily harm (ABH), wounding and inflicting grievous bodily harm (GBH) and causing GBH with intent — are contained in the Offences against the Person Act 1861.

Even at the time of its passing into law, the 1861 Act was rightly described as 'a rag-bag of offences' by its own draftsman, and as it is now nearly 150 years old, the criticisms are even more acute. Some of the language used is now archaic — 'grievous bodily harm' simply means serious harm, and 'assault occasioning actual bodily harm' most commonly means some kind of battery causing real harm to a victim. As to case law, the definition given to 'wounding' in *JCC* v *Eisenhower* (any breach in the outer and inner layers of the skin) is far too wide, as it could cover anything including a minor cut or even a graze. An interesting contrast can be made here with regard to the Theft Act 1968, which was intended to codify the entire law of theft. Within 10 years, a further Theft Act had to be passed and there have been significant statutory additions and amendments since. Yet the 1861 Act remains unamended (except by judicial interventions).

Other linguistic criticisms arise over the words 'assault' and 'battery'. Although 'assault' is technically used to describe 'causing a victim to fear the use of unlawful personal violence', it is most commonly understood to refer to some sort of physical attack. The strict definition of 'battery' is 'unlawful touching' and no injury of any sort is required.

 This is a very strong opening section explaining the most obvious criticisms of non-fatal offences. The comparison drawn between the 1861 Act and the Theft Act 1968 is interesting.

Probably the most serious criticism of the 1861 Act concerns the issue of *mens rea* for each of the offences. Section 47, which deals with assault occasioning ABH, is entirely silent on the issue of *mens rea*, and it has been left to the courts to determine what it is. The cases of *R* v *Savage* and *R* v *Parmenter* now confirm that the *mens rea* of assault or battery — intention or subjective recklessness — is all that is required. In s.20, the word 'malicious' has been interpreted to mean 'intention or recklessness as to causing some harm' (*R* v *Mowatt* and *R* v *Grimshaw*). In interpreting s.18, judges and academic lawyers have concluded that 'malicious' is effectively redundant, except as regards the secondary *mens rea* — intent to resist arrest.

 This is a good explanation of the two key *mens rea* problems in s.47 and s.20 offences.

A further point of criticism is that this Act is now undergoing almost perpetual revision and rewriting by judges, which could almost be called 'law-making by statutory interpretation'. The 2003 case of *R* v *Dica*, which involved a defendant being convicted of 'biological' GBH under s.20 after infecting two women with HIV, is another good example of the ability of senior courts to amend the law. The Court of Appeal, having quashed his conviction and ordered a retrial, confirmed that injury by reckless infection does constitute a s.20 offence and that *R* v *Clarence* (where a husband was prosecuted for infecting his wife with gonorrhoea) was overruled on the issue of direct bodily violence being required. (The more significant part of this judgement relates to the defence of consent, as the court ruled that if the victims knew or suspected that the defendant was infected, no criminal liability would arise.)

 This particular issue is not such an obvious one — until you understand how much case law is needed to 'make sense' of the 1861 Act.

Given the judicial decisions in *R* v *Savage* (s.47) and *R* v *Mowatt* (s.20), it is clear that these two offences now involve constructive liability — making it unnecessary for the Crown to prove intention or recklessness as to the *actus reus* of the offence. A conviction under s.47 can be obtained by proving that ABH was in fact caused by common assault and that the defendant either intended or was reckless as to the assault or battery. For neither of the offences is there a need to prove that the defendant intended or was reckless as to causing any level of harm at all. This issue of constructive liability militates against a basic principle of criminal liability called the principle of correspondence, which requires that the *mens rea* should be related to the *actus reus* of the offence and to the possible consequences of being convicted of that offence.

ⓔ This particular criticism is the most 'legal' of all and should always be included in such answers.

Finally, the 'hierarchy of sentencing' can easily be criticised. Both assault and battery have the same maximum sentence — 6 months. Section 47 ABH (for which only 'any hurt or injury which interferes with the health or comfort of the victim' needs to be proved) carries a maximum sentence 10 times that level — 5 years — which is exactly the same as that for s.20 wounding and inflicting GBH. These maximum sentences lack even a semblance of consistency or coherence.

It is evident that there is an indisputable case for the complete codification of the law on all non-fatal offences, but even the Law Commission's 1994 recommendations for reform did not include the common law offences of assault and battery. These recommended reforms included creating the following new offences: intentionally causing serious harm, recklessly causing serious harm and intentionally or recklessly causing some injury.

Although those recommendations have been welcomed by all governments since, no action has been taken to incorporate them into any of the major Criminal Justice Acts passed since.

ⓔ This section lacks some detail of the recommendations for reform and would therefore be marked as 'clear'.

ⓔ **24 or 25/25 marks awarded** (two sound sections, one clear section).

Section B

Question 1 Misrepresentation and breach of contract

Laura decided that she needed to lose some weight, so she paid £100 to Nell for ten 'weight loss' sessions. Nell's promotional material proclaimed her to be very experienced in running such sessions. It quoted a number of former participants as having been astonished and delighted by their weight losses. In fact, Nell was very much a beginner and she had made up the favourable quotes. After three sessions, Laura was dissatisfied with Nell's disorganised approach and unhelpful advice, and she decided that she wanted all of her money back.

Adapted from AQA examination paper, January 2006

Consider the rights and remedies available to Laura in connection with the 'weight loss' sessions. (25 marks)

ⓔ Questions often start with the word 'consider'. It is asking you to reflect on the circumstances in the scenario and to identify the relevant rules that might apply, based on the facts, and then to discuss how far the rules do apply.

A-grade answer

Nell's statements appear to be a misrepresentation, which is regarded in contract law as a vitiating factor, i.e. one that may invalidate the consent required for a contract to be binding. For a misrepresentation to be actionable, it has to fulfil three requirements:

- it must be untrue
- it must be a statement of fact not opinion (*Bissett* v *Wilkinson*)
- it must have induced the innocent party to enter into the contract

In the present case, it is immediately clear that the statements in the promotional material were untrue and it is equally clear that they purported to be statements of fact. They claimed that Nell was experienced in running weight-loss sessions, whereas she was in reality a beginner, and the quotes of former participants were invented.

There must be evidence that the misrepresentation induced the other party to enter the contract. In this case, it is difficult to see how Laura could have checked the truth of the statements. She quite clearly relied on them and she had no alternative source of information to use.

Contract law recognises three types of misrepresentation — fraudulent, negligent and innocent. Which category a misrepresentation falls into depends on the state of mind of the person making the statement. Fraudulent misrepresentation, also actionable as the tort of deceit, was defined in *Derry* v *Peek* as a false statement 'that is made (i) knowingly, or (ii) without belief in its truth, or (iii) recklessly as to whether it be true or false'. Negligent misrepresentation was established in the leading case of *Hedley Byrne* v *Heller Partners Ltd*, which established that a duty of care is created where there is a 'special relationship' between the parties and reliance is placed by one party on a statement given by the other. Today, however, the Misrepresentation Act 1967 is used much more widely in cases of negligent misrepresentation. In Nell's case, it is evident that the statements amounted to fraudulent misrepresentation because they had been deliberately invented. They were made in the full knowledge that they were false and so meet the criteria for fraudulent misrepresentation set out in *Derry* v *Peek*.

The effect of a misrepresentation is generally to make the contract voidable, so that it continues to exist unless and until the innocent party chooses to have it set aside by means of rescission, an equitable remedy, which puts the parties back in the position they were in before the contract was made. Rescission will not be ordered where it is impossible to return the parties to their original pre-contract position.

Affirmation of the contract, which means saying or doing something to indicate an intention to continue with it, is a bar to rescission. With fraudulent misrepresentation, however, the right to rescind will not be lost through what appears to be affirmation if the innocent party was not aware of the fraud and could not have been expected to discover it with reasonable diligence, because he or she would not have known that there was any right to rescind (*Peyman* v *Lanjani*). Laura did attend three sessions, which might indicate an intention to affirm the contract, but it could be argued that this was before her gradual dissatisfaction with Nell's performance gave her the idea that the promotional material might be fraudulent; she should not, therefore, lose the right to rescind.

Laura can also claim damages as a result of the misrepresentation for any losses (i.e. the £100 she has paid), which she has suffered as a direct consequence of it. Damages for misrepresentation are calculated on the same basis as they are in tort, so that the aim is to put the parties back in the position they were in before the misrepresentation was made.

ⓔ The coverage of misrepresentation is very thorough. Notice that the answer begins with establishing whether there has been a misrepresentation and only then does it consider what type of misrepresentation it might be. The answer also deals with remedies. Notice how the answer refers frequently to the circumstances outlined in the question and applies the rules to reach a conclusion.

It can be argued that Nell is in breach of contract because of her disorganised approach and unhelpful advice. Assuming that this does amount to a breach, Laura's rights will depend on the nature of the term that has been broken. A breach of a condition is a breach of an important term and gives the right to terminate the agreement and repudiate (cancel) the contract. Where the injured party elects to repudiate for a breach of condition, the general effect is to terminate the contract from the date of that election. A breach of warranty is a breach of a minor term that does not go to the root of the contract and gives rise only to a claim for damages. The distinction between conditions and warranties is illustrated by the cases of *Bettini* v *Gye* and *Poussard* v *Spiers and Pond*.

If Laura is able to establish that the breach went to the very root of the agreement and amounted to a breach of condition, she will be able to recover all the money paid, including that for future sessions, because she will be able to cancel the contract. However, if the court decides that the disorganisation and unhelpful advice amount only to breach of warranty, Laura will be able to claim only compensation for the poor quality of the sessions, which will probably be a proportion of the £30 paid for the three sessions she has had. She would not be entitled to cancel the sessions still to come, even though she may by now be unwilling to continue with the course.

e The section on breach is briefer, but the important elements are identified and applied to the facts. Students often neglect to deal with remedies in sufficient depth, but this answer outlines all the remedies available and considers the different possibilities that may arise.

e **23/25 marks awarded.** Overall this is a strong response.

Question 2 Frustration and breach of contract

Sue asked Paul to create a large banner to be the centrepiece of a forthcoming protest march on the theme of 'exploitation of animals through the ages'. She agreed to pay him £2,000 in total, £200 immediately and the remainder on completion and delivery of the banner. One month before delivery was due, Sue 'cancelled' the agreement because of financial difficulties and told Paul that she would not pay for the banner. By that time, the banner was almost finished and Paul had spent £400 on materials. He refused to accept the 'cancellation' and continued to work on the banner. A week before delivery was due, an order was made prohibiting all marches in the locality for 1 month because of fears that the protest march would provoke violence and disorder. In consequence, the protest march had to be abandoned.

Adapted from AQA examination paper, January 2006

Discuss the rights, duties and remedies of Paul and Sue arising out of the situation with the banner and the cancelled protest march. (25 marks)

e This question uses the word 'discuss', but it means the same as 'consider'. Notice that the question does not indicate which areas of law might be relevant. You are expected to identify these and this should always be the first thing you do. The question also asks you to discuss the rights, duties and remedies of two people.

A-grade answer

Sue seems to be in breach of contract when she 'cancels' the agreement. Her conduct amounts to anticipatory breach and Paul would be entitled to treat the contract as at an end and sue for damages. However, he opts to continue with the work. The injured party in an anticipatory breach of contract does have this option and can then sue for breach later, when the performance date has passed. This is what happened in

AQA A2 Law

Avery v *Bowden*, a case involving an agreement to supply a cargo for a ship at a port in Russia. Unfortunately, by the time the cargo was due, the contract had become frustrated because of the outbreak of the Crimean War, which made trading with Russia illegal. Paul could face a similar outcome if the court decides that the contract has been frustrated by the banning of the march. The issue of frustration is discussed later in this answer.

The innocent party may not always be able to insist on affirming the contract because, under the principle of mitigation of loss, he or she usually has a general duty to take reasonable steps to minimise the loss. In *White and Carter* v *McGregor*, the claimants opted to affirm the contract and the court upheld this decision, but added the provisos that it must be possible to carry out the contract without the other party's cooperation and that there must be a 'legitimate interest' in carrying on with the contract. In the present situation, it is possible for Paul to continue with the work without Sue's cooperation, and he would probably argue that there is a legitimate interest because there was not much he could have done to mitigate his loss, as the materials had already been bought and most of the work was already done. He should, therefore, be able to claim the full £2,000, provided he completes the banner and delivers it on time.

(e) The answer begins with breach of contract because this is the most obvious issue to arise in view of Sue's 'cancellation' of the agreement. It then goes on to consider the separate issue of frustration, which if established would result in a different outcome.

Sue may argue, however, that the contract has been frustrated because, a week before the banner was due to be delivered, an order was made prohibiting the march, of which the banner was to be the centrepiece. Frustration arises when an event occurs during the lifetime of a contract that is not the fault of either party and that makes completion of the contract impossible, illegal or radically different. The substance of the agreement itself has to be undermined and it is not sufficient that completion is made more difficult or expensive. A contract can also be frustrated if it is rendered impossible by the passing of a new statute, which makes the provisions of the contract illegal. This is not exactly the situation here. It is true that the march has been banned, but only for a month, and the banner would presumably be equally relevant to future marches in a few months' time. *Herne Bay Steam Boat* v *Sutton* is relevant here. Arguably, the banner continues to have a purpose even without the march. It could be displayed on other occasions and in a variety of circumstances. Given the fact that it cost £2,000, it seems unlikely that Sue intended it to be destroyed immediately after the march and never used again.

Her claim of frustration of contract seems unlikely to succeed, especially if the court takes account of the fact that she attempted to cancel the contract before the march had been banned. If it did succeed, however, Sue would be in a much better position than if she were in breach of contract. Under the Law Reform (Frustrated Contracts) Act 1943, all money is returned to where it was originally, allowing the court to apportion losses fairly between the parties so that they can each be reimbursed for expenses or for goods or services already obtained under the contract.

The issue here would be whether Sue has obtained a valuable benefit. One of the problems is to decide whether the valuable benefit is the work itself or the end product. In this case, the banner could be seen as valuable in itself and Sue will have the benefit of it in the future. It is possible, therefore, that, even if the contract is held to be frustrated, Sue will have to pay a substantial proportion of the £1,800 due on delivery of the banner in recognition of the valuable benefit she has obtained.

(e) This is a thorough and detailed answer, which outlines the relevant rules on both breach and frustration and makes good use of case authority. Notice how the answer uses the cases that seem to be the most relevant and applies them to the contract between Sue and Paul. Notice, too, how frequently the answer refers to the facts in the question. To get high marks, answers must outline relevant rules and apply them to the situation described in the scenario.

(e) 23/25 marks awarded.

Question 3 Formation of contract

Leroy wanted his kitchen painted and he knew that his friend Vince, who had recently retired, would be interested in doing it. He left a message on Vince's home telephone answering machine saying: 'I need my kitchen painted. Are you interested in doing it? Tell me "yes" or "no" by Tuesday. Leave a message if I am out.' Later that day, Vince sent a text message to Leroy's mobile phone telling him that he would do the painting. Leroy did not see the message until Friday. On Wednesday, Leroy met his neighbour William who was a painter and decorator and they started talking about Leroy's need to have his kitchen painted. Leroy had previously helped William with his accounts and William said that he would paint the kitchen 'as a favour for the help with the accounts as long as you buy me a pint'. Leroy agreed, but, despite several reminders, William failed to start the work and when finally challenged by Leroy he said that he was now too busy and that anyway he hadn't meant his offer to do the work to be taken seriously.

Consider the rights and remedies of Vince against Leroy and of Leroy against William in connection with the painting of the kitchen.   (25 marks)

(e) The question uses the word 'consider' and requires you to identify the relevant rules and apply them. It also asks you to deal with two separate situations.

Dealing first with Vince, it is necessary to identify whether there is a valid contract between him and Leroy. One issue is whether, in view of the fact that they were friends, there was an intention to create legal relations. The presumption that the arrangement is a purely social one will be rebutted if money has changed hands. The leading cases involving people other than family members — among them *Simpkins* v *Pays*, *Peck* v *Lateu* and *Parker* v *Clarke* — suggest that the courts will treat agreements between friends as contractual, so long as the actions of the parties suggest that they intended to form a legal agreement. This would seem to be the case here, because Leroy's conduct suggests that he was prepared to pay anyone who was willing to do the work.

But there also needs to be an offer and an acceptance. An offer can be defined as an expression of willingness to contract on certain terms, made with the intention that it will become binding on acceptance. It needs to be distinguished from an invitation to treat, which is an invitation to someone to make an offer. To be an offer, the terms must be certain and unambiguous. In *Guthing* v *Lynn*, the buyer of a horse promised to pay the seller an extra £5 'if the horse is lucky for me'. This was considered too vague to constitute an offer. The offer must be communicated so that its terms are known to the person accepting, and finally it must still be in existence when it is accepted. The difficulty with Leroy's statement is that it is not certain and unambiguous. It seems from the phrase 'Are you interested in doing it?' that he is simply making an initial enquiry, as in *Harvey* v *Facey,* rather than offering the work to Vince. So this would constitute an invitation to treat rather than an offer.

If Leroy's statement is regarded as an offer there is some uncertainty about whether Vince's reply would constitute a valid acceptance. To be valid, an acceptance must be an unqualified and unconditional agreement by words or conduct to all the terms of the offer. It is not clear whether Vince attempts to speak directly to Leroy, but he does send an unambiguous acceptance by text message 'later that day', which seems to be well within the deadline of Tuesday. It could be argued that, by saying 'Leave a message if I am out', Leroy is expecting a message on his home telephone, but this is not explicit and Vince can certainly argue that he has left a message. But if, as seems likely, Leroy's statement is an invitation to treat, Vince's text message would constitute an offer, which Leroy is free to reject.

ⓔ This is quite a complex question with several things to consider. The answer deals with offer and acceptance after intention to create legal relations, because this is the decisive issue in considering whether there is a contract between Leroy and Vince, but it would be equally valid to start with offer and acceptance.

The issue that arises in the negotiations with William is whether there is valid consideration. Consideration involves something of value being offered by each party. Sometimes it can be of little value, and it does not have to correspond to the actual worth of what the other party offers (*Chappell and Co. Ltd* v *Nestlé*). In principle therefore help with the accounts could constitute valid consideration for William painting the kitchen. But another rule is that to be valid, consideration must not be something that has been done in the past. Any consideration must come after the agreement, rather than being something that has already been done. In *Re McArdle* an agreement was not enforceable because the work had been done before the agreement was made. It is clear that the help with accounts cannot constitute valid consideration, but it could be argued that there is still a valid contract. In *Chappell* v *Nestlé*, chocolate bar wrappers were held to be good consideration and the promise to buy a pint would seem to be of sufficient economic value to amount to sufficient consideration.

If there is a valid contract and William refuses to carry out the work, Leroy can sue him for breach of contract and claim damages. The purpose of damages is to put the parties in the place they would have been in if the contract had been performed (*Robinson* v *Harman*). It is likely that any damages awarded would be on the basis of the cost of having the work done by someone else, but Leroy would have a duty to mitigate his loss. It is clear from *British Westinghouse* v *Underground Electric Railways* that he would be expected to do what the reasonable and prudent person would do, which would be to have the work done to the same standard as would have been expected from William.

ⓔ Notice that the answer is quite sparing in the amount of detail it gives and the focus is on applying the relevant rules of offer/acceptance, intention to create legal relations and consideration. Note that the question also asks about remedies so there is some discussion of this at the end.

ⓔ **23 or 24/25 marks awarded.** The answer covers the important issues and refers to appropriate authorities. There is application to the facts throughout.

Question 4 Sale of Goods Act, exclusion clauses and privity of contract

Alan bought an adjustable garden chair from Garden Products. He told the sales assistant that he intended it as a surprise present for his sister Katherine and he arranged for it to be delivered to her address. Katherine used the chair several times without incident, but after about a month a support fractured when she was using it in the upright position and it suddenly collapsed, throwing her sharply backwards. As a result she wrenched her back and was unable to work as a dance instructor for 5 weeks. There was a clause on the invoice which said that defects had to be reported within 2 weeks of purchase and that liability was limited to the value of the product.

Consider any possible rights and remedies Katherine may have against Garden Products in connection with the sale of the chair and the injury she suffered.

(25 marks)

ⓔ The question uses the word 'consider' and requires you to identify the relevant rules and apply them. Notice that you are asked to consider the rules in connection with the sale of the chair — this is a clue that the focus will be on the sale of goods. The other point to note is that while it was Alan who bought the chair, the question asks about Katherine's rights, so you will need to consider the rights that third parties have.

A-grade answer

This is a contract for the sale of goods, and the implied terms in the Sale of Goods Act 1979 are therefore applicable to it. Under s.14(2) there is an implied term that goods are of satisfactory quality. This term applies only to sales in the course of a business and not to private sales, but they will apply to this sale because Garden Products is clearly a business. Under Section 14(2)(a), goods are satisfactory if 'they meet the standard that a reasonable person would regard as satisfactory, taking account of any description of the goods, the price (if relevant) and all other relevant circumstances'. In *Bartlett* v *Sidney Marcus* (1965), the court said that a second-hand car did not have to be in perfect condition and some defects were to be expected. However, the garden chair in this question is clearly new and Alan would therefore expect it to be without defect.

Among the potentially relevant factors outlined under s.14(2)(b) to determine what is meant by satisfactory quality are safety and durability. In *Priest* v *Last*, a hot-water bottle burst. It was clearly neither safe nor durable. Here we are told that, after Katherine had used the chair several times it suddenly collapsed, presumably as a result of the support fracturing. This would suggest that there is an issue with durability because supports should not fracture after such a short period. The fracture led to an accident and so the chair, like the hot-water bottle in *Priest* v *Last*, is not safe and therefore not of satisfactory quality.

Section 14(3) states that there is an implied term that goods are fit for any purpose specifically made known to the seller, unless the buyer does not rely on the seller's judgement or it would be unreasonable for him or her to do so. There is no suggestion in this case that that the chair was being used for an unusual purpose and therefore there is an expectation that it is fit for the purpose for which garden chairs are normally sold. There would, therefore, be a breach of s.14(2) as well as s.14(3), as there was in *Priest* v *Last*.

ⓔ There are a number of different issues to be considered in this question. It requires discussion of the Sale of Goods Act implied terms, the remedies available under the Act and the issue of acceptance. Notice how the answer covers these elements and how effectively it uses case authority to try to assess how the rules would be applied.

Because the implied terms are conditions, Alan has the right to reject the contract as well as to claim damages. However under s.11(4) of the 1979 Act, this right to reject is lost once the goods have been accepted and the claim would then be limited to damages. The Sale and Supply of Goods Act 1994 amended the 1979 Act and redefined when acceptance takes place. Under the 1994 Act the buyer must have reasonable opportunity to examine the goods.

In this case it is unclear whether the chair would be treated as accepted because Katherine used it 'several times' over a period of a month, but, in any event, the claim here will also involve damages, which will always be a remedy, whether the goods have been accepted or not. Damages are appropriate where, as in this case, consumers have suffered personal injury because of a faulty product and wish to sue for consequential loss. The consumer will often be awarded sums far exceeding the value of the product itself. For example in *Godley* v *Perry*, £2,500 was awarded for the loss of an eye caused by a faulty catapult. The claim here would be for loss of earnings.

We are also told that the invoice contained a clause stating that Garden Products only accepted liability for defects reported within 2 weeks of purchase. Under s.6 of the Unfair Contract Terms Act 1977, the terms in s.14 of the Sale of Goods Act 1979 cannot be excluded from consumer contracts. Applying s.12(1) of the 1977 Act, Alan is clearly buying as a consumer, so any limitation clause cannot exclude the implied terms or place restrictions on consumers' statutory rights. The clause on the invoice tries to do this by limiting claims to defects which are reported within 2 weeks of purchase and to the value of the product itself and it would therefore be void.

ⓔ The answer considers the impact of the limitation clause, but coverage is brief because there are so many other issues to discuss.

The final issue that needs to be discussed is the fact that it is Katherine who is injured, rather than the purchaser of the chair. Only parties to a contract can sue under it and Katherine was given the chair as a present. However, the Contracts (Rights of Third Parties) Act 1999 creates certain exceptions to the general rule of privity of contract. Under s.1(1), the Act allows a third party to enforce a contract if it contains an express term to that effect or if it purports to confer a benefit on him or her. The Act allows enforcement only where the benefit is intended for a specific person or for a member of a specific group and where it is clear that the parties intended the benefit to be enforceable by the third party. We are told that Alan told the sales assistant at Garden Products that the chair was for Katherine, and arranged for it to be delivered to her address. The provisions of the Act would therefore apply and Katherine will be able to sue under the contract.

ⓔ Finally, the answer deals with the fact that it is Katherine who is injured while using the chair, when she was not a party to the contract.

ⓔ **25/25 marks awarded.** A lot is expected of students on this question, and in the time available, it is difficult to see how an answer could cover much more than this response does.

Question 5 Critical evaluation of law on offer and acceptance

> **What criticisms could be made of the current rules on offer and acceptance and what reforms might be appropriate?**
>
> (25 marks)

ⓔ This is a very different kind of question from the others. In asking you to identify criticisms and possible reforms it is asking you to evaluate the law. It requires you to comment critically on the various rules.

A-grade answer

The rules on offer and acceptance have been developed by the courts over many years, and the fact that there has been no need for statutory intervention suggests that, on the whole, they have worked well. However, there are a number of criticisms that can be made of specific aspects.

One long-standing concern is the relationship between offers and invitations to treat. An offer can be defined as an expression of willingness to contract on certain terms, made with the intention that it will become binding on acceptance. On the face of it, goods advertised in shop windows would seem to comply with this definition. However, goods in shop windows are invitations to treat, not offers. The case of *Fisher* v *Bell* — where a shopkeeper was prosecuted for displaying an illegal flick-knife for sale in his shop window and acquitted because an exhibition of goods in a shop window is not an offer for sale — illustrates the confusion this can cause. It could be argued that the outcome was unsatisfactory because the shopkeeper clearly intended to sell the knife and he would have sold it to anyone who came in with the right money. Equally clearly, Parliament intended to criminalise exactly this kind of behaviour.

One consequence of the current law on offers and invitations is that, in retail situations, the seller retains ultimate control over who to sell to. This is based on the principle of freedom of contract, and Professor Sir Percy Winfield made a case for it in a 1939 article in the *Law Quarterly Review*, arguing that 'a shop is a place for bargaining and not compulsory sales'. Decisions such as *Pharmaceutical Society* v *Boots* follow this principle.

There is still confusion in some areas, for example with timetables and tickets for transport. In *Wilkie* v *London Passenger Transport Board* (1947), it was suggested that the offer is made by running the service, and acceptance is when the passenger gets on board, but in *Contract Law* Elliott and Quinn suggest that, if the principles laid down in *Thornton* v *Shoe Lane Parking* (1971) are followed, it would appear that passengers asking for a ticket are making an invitation to treat, that the bus company makes an offer by issuing the ticket and that the passenger accepts the offer by keeping the ticket without objection.

Another area of potential difficulty is distinguishing offers from responses to requests for further information. In *Harvey* v *Facey*, it was held that, following the appellants' telegram to Facey, reading 'Will you sell us Bumper Hall Pen? Telegraph lowest cash

price — answer paid', Facey's reply (a telegram reading 'Lowest price for Bumper Hall Pen £900') was not an offer but merely a statement of the price. The courts have adopted quite a narrow interpretation of what constitutes an offer when information is being supplied. For example, in *Gibson* v *Manchester City Council* (1979), a statement that the council 'may be prepared to sell the house to you' at a certain price was held to be an invitation to treat, not an offer.

Acceptance in unilateral contracts is another difficulty because acceptance can be through conduct, so it may not always be clear when performance constituting acceptance has started. Where a substantial amount of work has been done by an offeree, it would not seem fair to allow the offeror to revoke the offer. As a solution to this, the Law Commission in 1975 suggested that an offer that the offeror has said will be open for a specific period should not be revocable within that period.

There is also the issue of the 'postal rule', which applies when ordinary letter post is used and means that acceptance is valid when posted, even if the letter is lost in the post, but a revocation of an offer is valid only when it is received. These days, fewer and fewer contracts are being entered into by letter, so the postal rule will become less relevant, but there may still be situations — such as delivery by courier — where it would apply. The main problem with the postal rule is that the offeror may not know of the acceptance, for example if the letter disappears in the post. In *Re London and Northern Bank* (1900), it was held that a letter is posted if it is correctly addressed and stamped and placed in an official post box; this at least suggests that an incorrectly addressed letter would not constitute acceptance.

The broader issue is whether the postal rule is any longer appropriate in view of the other means of communication now available. In the twenty-first century, a person accepting an offer can easily check whether any e-mailed or posted acceptance has been received, possibly using an instantaneous method of communication, such as the telephone or fax. It would be more consistent to have a rule that makes acceptance valid only when it is received. Another issue is that, even when it is delivered, a letter opened in the front office may not be seen by an intended recipient until much later.

Further problems relating to acceptance arise with the use of electronic communications, which are transmitted instantaneously. Denning LJ in the *Entores* case suggested that the burden should rest with the person accepting the offer to make sure that his or her communication has been received. For example, if the telephone goes dead, there is a need to telephone again.

One interesting point is that there has been no definitive ruling on when an acceptance is made using e-mails. One approach is that the postal rule should apply and the acceptance becomes valid when 'send' is pressed, but it has been argued that the *Entores* rule should apply so that the sender would have the responsibility to check that the e-mail has been received. As with letters, there is no guarantee that the e-mail has been opened and read. It does seem unsatisfactory that there is no definitive ruling on this by the courts and this would seem to be one obvious area for reform.

No comprehensive proposals for reform have been made. This is an area of law where Parliament has not found it necessary to intervene because the courts have been able to adapt the existing rules to suit changing circumstances. EU regulations now cover internet contracts and it seems likely that future reform will also come from the EU.

ⓔ This is a thorough answer which discusses a range of criticisms. It also comments briefly on possible reforms, though it makes the point that few actual reform proposals have been made. Notice that it concentrates heavily on evaluation and refers to the rules only when an evaluative comment is made. The danger with this question is that the answer may become a summary of the rules, with little evaluative comment, but this answer avoids that trap.

ⓔ **24/25 marks awarded.**

Knowledge check answers

1 That the jury may find the defendant had the necessary intention for murder if they believe that he or she recognised that death or serious injury was a virtually certain consequence of his or her voluntary acts.

2 Homicide Act 1957 s.2.

3 Abnormality of mental functioning that arose from a recognised medical condition which substantially impaired the defendant's ability to understand the nature of the defendant's conduct or to form a rational judgement or to exercise self-control.

4 That the alcoholism had to have caused an abnormality of mental functioning or that 'the defendant's craving for drink had to be such as to render the defendant's use of drink involuntary because he was no longer able to resist the impulse to drink'.

5 The defendant's fear of serious violence from the victim or another identified person, or 'things done or said (or both) which (a) constituted circumstances of an extremely grave character, and (b) caused D to have a justifiable sense of being seriously wronged'. The final trigger is a combination of the 'fear' and 'anger' triggers.

6 Because with provocation there was no minimum threshold laid down for provoking conduct. Now under the new rules, the defendant must prove that the circumstances must be not merely grave, but extremely so and also it is not enough that the defendant has been caused by the circumstances to feel a sense of grievance. It must arise from a justifiable sense not merely that he or she has been wronged, but that he or she has been seriously wronged.

7 The jury finally has to decide whether a person of the defendant's sex and age, with a normal degree of tolerance and self-restraint and in the circumstances of the defendant, might have reacted in the same or in a similar way to the defendant.

8 The three types of involuntary manslaughter are:
- manslaughter by an unlawful and dangerous act
- manslaughter by gross negligence
- reckless manslaughter

9 R v Franklin.

10 The 'unlawful act must be such as all sober and reasonable people would inevitably recognise must subject the other person to, at least, the risk of some harm resulting therefrom, albeit not serious harm'.

11 R v Singh.

12 Because in Richardson, the patient had consented to the dental work and there was no deception by the appellant, whereas in Tabassum the victim did not know the quality of the act of the defendant and therefore could not validly consent to it.

13 It was held that the fact that the injury had occurred as a result of foul play was not sufficient to negate consent and accordingly, to convict the defendant. The jury would have to consider other relevant factors such as the degree of force used, the extent of the risk of injury and the state of mind of the accused.

14 At the time of the committing of the act, the defendant was labouring under such a defect of reason, from disease of the mind, as not to know the nature and quality of the act he was doing, or, if he did know it, that he did not know he was doing what was wrong.

15 'Any mental disorder which has manifested itself in violence and is prone to recur is a disease of the mind'.

16 Because when he stated 'I suppose they will hang me for this', it proved he knew that killing his wife was legally wrong and therefore he was not legally insane under the M'Naghten rules.

17 Because the cause of the defendant's loss of control was internal — his failure to take sufficient insulin.

18 That the force used was both necessary and reasonable.

19 R v Williams.

20 R v Majewski and R v Lipman.

21 R v Burstow.

22 Where there is no correspondence between the actus reus and mens rea of an offence — the mens rea of a lesser offence is 'constructed' into that required for a more serious offence.

23 R v Vickers.

24 That the circumstances must be extremely grave and the defendant's sense of grievance must arise from a justifiable sense of being seriously wronged.

25 R v Clegg.

26 Winterwerp v Netherlands.

27 An offer is defined as an expression of willingness to contract on certain terms, made with the intention that it will become binding on acceptance.

28 Hyde v Wrench.

29 Acceptance is immediate as long as the message is received.

30 A promise to do something in the future.

31 It allows a third party to enforce a contract if it contains an express term to that effect or if the contract purports to confer a benefit on a third party.

32 A term is a statement which is incorporated into the contract and forms part of it. A representation is a statement intended to persuade a party to enter a contract.

33 A breach of a condition will give the injured party the choice of either repudiating (ending) the contract or continuing with it and claiming damages, whereas a breach of warranty entitles the injured party only to damages.

34 Goods are of satisfactory quality if they meet the standard that a reasonable person would regard as satisfactory, taking account of any description of the goods, the price (if relevant) and all the other relevant circumstances.

35 It allows the purchaser to reject the goods and demand the return of the purchase price.

36 Unfair Contract Terms Act 1977.

37 A misrepresentation is an untrue statement of fact that induces a party to enter a contract but is not itself part of the contract.

38 It brings it automatically to an end.

39 To place the injured party, so far as money can do it, in the same situation as if the contract had been performed.